Lean Product
Management

Successful products from fuzzy
business ideas

Mangalam Nandakumar

BIRMINGHAM - MUMBAI

Lean Product Management

Acquisition Editors: Ben Renow-Clarke, Suresh Jain

Project Editor: Radhika Atitkar

Technical Editor: Nidhisha Shetty

Proofreader: Tom Jacob

Indexer: Rekha Nair

Graphics: Sandip Tadge

Production Coordinator: Sandip Tadge

First published: May 2018

Production reference: 1300518

Published by Packt Publishing Ltd.

Livery Place

35 Livery Street

Birmingham B3 2PB, UK.

ISBN 978-1-78883-117-8

www.packtpub.com

mapt.io

Mapt is an online digital library that gives you full access to over 5,000 books and videos, as well as industry leading tools to help you plan your personal development and advance your career. For more information, please visit our website.

Why subscribe?

- Spend less time learning and more time coding with practical eBooks and Videos from over 4,000 industry professionals
- Learn better with Skill Plans built especially for you
- Get a free eBook or video every month
- Mapt is fully searchable
- Copy and paste, print, and bookmark content

PacktPub.com

Did you know that Packt offers eBook versions of every book published, with PDF and ePub files available? You can upgrade to the eBook version at www.PacktPub.com and as a print book customer, you are entitled to a discount on the eBook copy. Get in touch with us at service@ packtpub.com for more details.

At www.PacktPub.com, you can also read a collection of free technical articles, sign up for a range of free newsletters, and receive exclusive discounts and offers on Packt books and eBooks.

Contributors

About the author

Mangalam Nandakumar has over 17 years of experience in product management and software delivery. She is an entrepreneur and has founded two start-ups. She has worked at Citigroup, Ocwen Financial Solutions, ThoughtWorks Technologies, and RangDe.Org. Mangalam presents a vibrant perspective on product management from her diverse experience of working with start-ups, enterprises, and nonprofits, both in product companies and software consultancy organizations. She has a strong foundation in Agile and Lean methodologies. She has also coached teams on their Agile transformation journeys.

Mangalam started her career as a programmer and soon transitioned to business analysis and product management. She has consulted for businesses in various functional domains and has helped them articulate their product vision, strategy, and roadmap. She has led many software teams through successful product deliveries. Mangalam cofounded her start-up, AIDAIO, in 2014, to enable businesses to enhance their customer engagement strategies. AIDAIO was shortlisted under the Top 10 Promising Start-Ups by CII in 2015. Moreover, AIDAIO's innovative platform to design, build, and launch white-labeled native iOS and Android apps for events and conference was a finalist in the Best Event Technology category at MICE Asia Pacific, 2015.

Mangalam has also spoken at various conferences on topics related to Agile and product management. She started her writing journey by blogging on topics related to product management, team processes, and diversity at workplaces. She is passionate about mentoring women and is a vocal advocate for diversity at workplaces. She was instrumental in founding organization-level initiatives to coach and guide women to speak at conferences. Mangalam is also an artist and paints in various mediums. She ran an art school and has conducted art workshops as well as exhibited and sold her artworks. She lives in Bengaluru, India and enjoys playing and watching movies with her son.

Writing this book has been a dream come true for me. It has been harder, but more enjoyable than I thought. It took a lot of encouragement, patience, and support from everyone—family, friends, and colleagues to make this happen. This is such a special milestone for me, and I want to thank everyone who helped to make this book a reality.

First, to my dearest little boy, Siddharth. You compiled your first book when you were eight. You're my inspiration and my superhero! Thanks for encouraging me to write, for giving me my space and reviewing all the quotes in the book. Thanks for all the hugs too. You keep me going.

Mom and Dad, thanks for always believing in me. I could never have made it this far without your unconditional support and love. You taught me to aim high and never settle for less.

Jaiku, Uma, Viku, and Shruti, thanks for always cheering me on and for making me feel special. To my besties, Arundhati, Sujata, and Subhashri. Thank you for always being there for me. To Gru, for being my sounding board and helping me think through my ideas. Thank you for your immense patience.

To Preethi Madhu, thanks for being my mentor, and showing me the path when I needed it the most. To Nishant, thanks for introducing me to the publishers. Thanks to all my colleagues, past, and present. I have learnt so much from you.

Finally, I want to thank the publishers, reviewers, and the editors for all your valuable comments, feedback, and suggestions. Your inputs have helped me articulate my views better and bring this book to the great shape it is today.

About the reviewer

Greg Cohen is a 20-year product management veteran with extensive experience in understanding customer needs and collaborating with development to create market-driven products. He is an expert and strong advocate of customer-centric design and agile development, and a pioneer in applying lean methods to product management.

Greg earned an MBA with honors from Babson College and a Bachelor of Science in Mechanical Engineering with second major in Electrical Engineering from Tufts University.

Greg is the founder of Agile Excellence LLC. He has worked and consulted for venture start-ups and large companies alike, including Software-as-a-Service (SaaS) products, data analytics, and medical diagnostics and devices.

Greg is the author of the books, *Strategy Excellence for Product Managers, Agile Excellence Press* (2017), *Agile Excellence for Product Managers, Super Star Press* (2010), and *42 Rules of Product Management, Super Star Press* (2013). He is the former President of the Silicon Valley Product Management Association as well as a speaker and frequent commentator on product management issues.

Packt is Searching for Authors Like You

If you're interested in becoming an author for Packt, please visit authors. packtpub.com and apply today. We have worked with thousands of developers and tech professionals, just like you, to help them share their insight with the global tech community. You can make a general application, apply for a specific hot topic that we are recruiting an author for, or submit your own idea.

TABLE OF CONTENTS

Part Two: Are we building the right product?

Part Three: Are we building the product right?

Preface

Product managers need to have the skill to step between a blurry 30,000 feet view and a close-up fine-grained view. Today, businesses are competing to innovate. Cost is no longer the constraint. Execution is. When competitive advantage for business is paramount, customer delight is non-negotiable, opportunities for impact are abound, product managers have to improvise on their strategy every day. The need to be Agile is about responding to abstract feedback from an ever shifting market. This book is about finding the smartest way to build an Impact Driven Product that can deliver value to customers and meet business outcomes when operating under internal and external constraints.

When starting on a new product, it can be quite hard to determine which product idea to pursue. Is there an objective metric to compare an idea's value? How can we factor engagement from all aspects of the business to create an impactful end-to-end product experience?

The book introduces the concept of investing in Key Business Outcomes as part of the product strategy. It can help elicit the stakeholder's investment in the execution of an idea. The book is a handy guide for product managers and for anyone embarking on a new product development to align their product strategy with business outcomes and customer impact.

Who this book is for

If you are leading a team that is building a new product, then this book is for you. The book is targeted at product managers, functional leads in enterprises, business sponsors venturing into new product offerings, product development teams, and start-up founders.

What this book covers

Part 1 – Defining what to build, who we are building for, and why

This part guides the reader to define the Impact Driven Product starting from the business model and working down to the details of Key Business Outcomes, customer value, success metrics and cost versus impact for every feature.

Chapter 1, Identify Key Business Outcomes, addresses defining the business model, understand Key Business Outcomes and defining an Impact Driven Product.

Chapter 2, Invest in Key Business Outcomes, introduces the concept of investing in Key Business Outcomes and the value of business agility in product development.

Chapter 3, Identify the Solution and its Impact on Key Business Outcomes, introduces the concept of feature ideas in a product backlog and introduces a framework to evaluate/prioritize ideas based on the estimated impact on Key Business Outcomes.

Chapter 4, Plan for Success, addresses the need to define a shared view of success and how to define success criteria for feature ideas.

Chapter 5, Identify the Impact Driven Product, introduces value mapping by defining impact scores and understanding risks and costs of a product feature.

Part 2 - Are we building the right product?

This part guides the reader to define the right metrics to effectively measure product progress and performance.

Chapter 6, Managing the Scope of an Impact Driven Product, addresses the limitations of a Minimum Viable Product and the need to think about the end-to-end product experience when defining product feature scope.

Chapter 7, Track, Measure, and Review Customer Feedback, addresses the importance of customer feedback and feedback channels and how to incorporate feedback into the product backlog.

Chapter 8, *Tracking Our Progress*, addresses how we can track product performance by measuring qualitative and quantitative metrics and also understanding the impact of metrics on product strategy.

Part 3 - Are we building the product right?

This part guides the reader to understand and identify processes that hold product teams from delivering maximum value and why it is important for product teams to discard wasteful processes and stay lean.

Chapter 9, *Eliminate Waste – Don't Estimate!*, addresses some common pitfalls of software estimations and the need for teams to embrace/discard the need for estimations based on product context.

Chapter 10, *Eliminate Waste – Don't Build What We Can Buy*, addresses the importance of building what the customer values the most – feature black holes that eat up a team's time and parameters to consider to enable a build versus buy decision.

Chapter 11, *Eliminate Waste – Data Versus Opinions*, explains the importance for product teams to have a data strategy, common pitfalls with data, and the importance of data driven decision making.

Chapter 12, *Is Our Process Dragging Us Down?*, addresses the typical process bottlenecks and offers guidelines to overcome these process bottlenecks.

Chapter 13, *Team Empowerment*, addresses why team empowerment is important for building successful products and what an empowered product team looks like.

To get the most out of this book

Familiarity with Lean Canvas, User Story Maps, Agile principles can help, but are not impediments to the reader.

Download the color images

We also provide a PDF file that has color images of the screenshots/diagrams used in this book. You can download it here:

```
https://www.packtpub.com/sites/default/files/
downloads/LeanProductManagement_ColorImages.pdf
```

Get in touch

Feedback from our readers is always welcome.

General feedback: Email feedback@packtpub.com, and mention the book's title in the subject of your message. If you have questions about any aspect of this book, please email us at questions@packtpub.com.

Errata: Although we have taken every care to ensure the accuracy of our content, mistakes do happen. If you have found a mistake in this book we would be grateful if you would report this to us. Please visit, http://www.packtpub.com/submit-errata, selecting your book, clicking on the Errata Submission Form link, and entering the details.

Piracy: If you come across any illegal copies of our works in any form on the Internet, we would be grateful if you would provide us with the location address or website name. Please contact us at copyright@packtpub.com with a link to the material.

If you are interested in becoming an author: If there is a topic that you have expertise in and you are interested in either writing or contributing to a book, please visit http://authors.packtpub.com.

Reviews

Please leave a review. Once you have read and used this book, why not leave a review on the site that you purchased it from? Potential readers can then see and use your unbiased opinion to make purchase decisions, we at Packt can understand what you think about our products, and our authors can see your feedback on their book. Thank you!

For more information about Packt, please visit packtpub.com.

— PART ONE —

DEFINING WHAT TO BUILD, WHO WE ARE BUILDING FOR, AND WHY

1

IDENTIFY KEY
BUSINESS
OUTCOMES

Modern product development is witnessing a drastic shift. Disruptive ideas and ambiguous businesses conditions have changed the way that products are developed. Product development is no longer guided by existing processes or predefined frameworks. Delivering on time is a baseline metric, as is software quality. Today, businesses are competing to innovate. They are willing to invest in groundbreaking products with cutting-edge technology. Cost is no longer the constraint—execution is. Can product managers then continue to rely upon processes and practices aimed at traditional ways of product building? How do we ensure that software product builders look at the bigger picture and do not tie themselves to engineering practices and technology viability alone? Understanding the business and customer context is essential for creating valuable products.

This chapter addresses the following topics:

- Defining our business model and unique value proposition
- Deriving inputs for product development
- Understanding Key Business Outcomes
- Defining our Impact Driven Product

We are driven by purpose

Honeycombs are an engineering marvel. The hexagonal shape of honeycombs is optimized to reduce the amount of wax needed to construct the hive, while maximizing the storage capacity. However, building wonderfully crafted honeycombs isn't the raison d'être of the bees. The goal of their existence is to maximize their chances of survival, to keep their lineage alive. Every bee activity is centered around this.

The need to maximize chances of survival is true for nearly every living species, but that does not mean that the queen of the ants should ask her ant army to construct ant hills with wax in hexagonal tubes. It doesn't work that way. Every species has an integral DNA that defines what it eats, how it socializes, how it defends or attacks, how it adapts, and how it survives.

The engineering that went into the honeycomb contributes to a specific way of life that is suited to the bees. It is important to realize that the very first bees didn't initially build wax hexagonal tubes. They iterated over many generations and responded to feedback from nature (which is often harsh and can result in extinction). Bees have pivoted to this model and it seems to have worked rather well for them. Heck, they've even managed to find channel partners in humans!

In the product world, understanding outcomes and user goals is essential to building successful products. A product's success always relates to the end goals it meets. Engineering in isolation adds no business value. The same can be said about marketing or sales. Business functions acting in isolation, without the context of business outcomes or creating value to the customer, are not sustainable. The sooner we define end goals, the better for the business as a whole. After all, we don't want to end up building honeycombs for ants.

Business context defines everything we do

> *"Universal law is for lackeys. Context is for kings."*
> *— Captain Lorca, Star Trek: Discovery.*

When the Agile manifesto was created in 2001, software practitioners were calling for a change in the way that software was delivered. The waterfall model of software development, which was predominant, required that software specifications and business requirements were frozen upfront. There was very little room for change. Change had to be avoided because changing anything midway would increase costs and timelines. Waterfall had evolved as a way to handle software development processes based on the limitations of the software technology of that time. Much of software development then was about automating manual processes or building bespoke technology solutions. Technology has since evolved a lot. It has become increasingly flexible and inexpensive to build technology solutions with direct consumer impact. The focus for software builders has expanded to include customer satisfaction and is no longer about just meeting budgets and timelines.

There are many frameworks (Scrum, XP, and so on.) that offer a methodology for software teams to focus on user experience and customer value. They foster team collaboration and enable teams to respond to change. The guiding principles behind these frameworks are noble, but failures always happen in how these principles are put into practice.

Without context, intent, and outcomes being defined, even well-meant advice can go waste. This is because we're humans and not honeybees. We are driven by purpose, we are lazy and we are imaginative. People can conjure up images of success (or failure) where there is none. They plan, speculate, and adapt. They try to optimize for imagined future situations. We know that a sense of purpose is crucial to rallying a group of diverse, independent, and creative people to come together and effect change (or even build great products). The problem is this is exactly where we seem to fail time and again.

We fail because we focus on the wrong stuff. We try to predictably measure productivity in a creative profession. We over-engineer solutions to nonexistent use cases. Software engineering is an interesting field of work. It's like an artist and a mathematician coming together to generate business value! Yet, we treat software engineering like automobile manufacturing. I know amazing software engineers who can churn out beautiful and working software, but their pace of delivery is not predictable. Every person has their own pace, and style of working, which is a problem for *project* managers. When we have strict timelines and budgets to meet, how do we commit if there is so much subjectivity? Software teams have spent a lot of time inventing processes to accurately predict engineering efforts. Estimations, planning activities, functional scoping, and progress reporting have gained a lot of visibility in this context. We focus too much on engineering practices.

Software product development is missing out on a great opportunity here. By carrying over software delivery frameworks of meeting timelines, budgets, and customer satisfaction, we are in a way restricting ourselves to looking at outputs instead of outcomes. It is time that we changed our perspective on this. Product management shouldn't be about measuring effort or productivity. Product management shouldn't be about measuring output. Instead we should focus on product outcomes. What value are we creating for the customer? What outcomes is the product helping the business to meet? How can we execute a plan to achieve this in the smartest way possible? So how do we measure these outcomes?

What influences product success?

In the good old days of business process automation (until late 1990s), measuring success seemed much simpler. Software teams could say, "There is an existing way of doing things. Let's automate that, but stick to budgets, timelines and quality metrics." Goals were simple and measurable. Software design was never discussed. User experience was nonexistent. Business impact was purely profitability based and no behavior changes were hinted at. Even as we moved into the era of Agile, business folks would give us weird looks when we asked to speak to end users. A client once told me, rather dismissively, "We're building this (app) for accountants. They don't have an eye for color. I don't know why you're worried about user interface or design." He may have made total sense a decade ago.

Today, you'll easily hear a CEO say things like, "We need to create stickiness, and to ingrain in our users a desire to engage with our apps." Many a product manager will roll their eyes and think, "Whatever that means." Success for a product is no longer about meeting budgets or timelines. The narrative of software development has changed. Can product management afford to lag behind?

Understanding business goals and evaluating risks and costs have always been essential for driving trade-off decisions. Business goals today are multidimensional and so are risks. How we make trade-off decisions depends on what aspects of product success we want to consider. Today, a product manager has to handle many facets of goals and risks, before defining the right product to build and driving trade-off decisions. According to the management consulting firm, McKinsey & Company, "Product managers are the glue that bind the many functions that touch a product—engineering, design, customer success, sales, marketing, operations, finance, legal, and more. They not only own the decisions about what gets built but also influence every aspect of how it gets built and launched."

Traditional *project planning* isn't going to help anymore. Product managers are in the driver's seat. We have to steer the product to meet ambiguous business goals. When building disruptive products in ambiguous business conditions, there is no "existing way" to refer to. All we have is a bunch of glorious ideas. So, the first step to demystifying goals is to articulate intent.

Impact Driven Product development needs to consider four key pieces of input that influence and guide product success:

- Business outcomes that a product can deliver. Why is this product important for the business?
- Value that a product can create for a customer. What should we build in order to deliver the maximum value to users?
- Execution plan. When there are many ways to implement the same functionality, how do we decide upon the best way forward?
- Internal business constraints and external market influences.

A business as a whole has its own value creation goals outlined. A product may address some or all of a business' goals.

A business model

A business model is a starting point for identifying a product idea and drawing up a plan. The desired outcome of this plan is to identify the unique value proposition that our business intends to deliver to the users/customers. In order to arrive at this, we need to define who our users are, what problems we're trying to solve, what channels we can leverage, who our competition is, how we plan to make our revenues, and what costs we might incur.

For start-ups, or businesses in the early stages of development, Lean Canvas, or any other framework that can help to visualize the market, business ecosystem, unique value proposition, and target segments, is a great place to start. Even for a product manager joining a team midway through product development, understanding the vision, market and target groups, and so on is key. After all, context is king. If the business model hasn't yet been laid out, then I recommend that you do that first.

Lean Canvas is a fantastic tool for capturing the business model around a product. Product Vision Board is also another tool to help us to visualize the product vision. Defining the business model around the product is a great way to define the target customers, the problems we're trying to solve for them, and the unique value proposition that we can offer. This can form the basis of how we want to run our business. Not every aspect of our business needs to be productized. Also, not every user segment may value every product feature with equal merit.

The business model can help us to visualize these target segments and capture which segments we want to go after in the current phase of business. However, Lean Canvas stops at the business model level. When investing in technology, we need to be clear about the outcomes we seek and the trade-offs we need to make. Building a product requires that we understand the larger business context, but we iterate on a product strategy that helps us to deliver a solution that meets business outcomes and provides value to customers. Software technology is extremely flexible. We can build quick and dirty solutions, or we can build robust, long-lasting solutions. However, every product must be based on business and customer motivations, and not on technology preferences.

The following is the Lean Canvas model proposed by *Ash Maurya*:

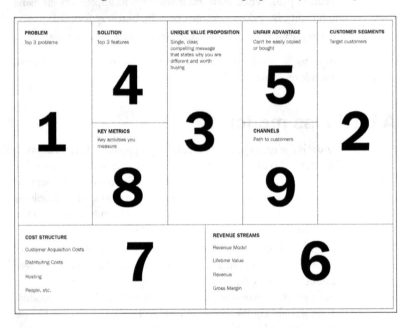

The overall business plan may also vary depending on the stage of the business. Business context and constraints have a bearing on what is achievable. For instance, at early stages, a business may be interested in creating value for early adopters. Some businesses may not attach importance to revenue generation until there is sufficient traction. As a business scales, other goals may become important. Value creation becomes more comprehensive.

This relationship between business outcomes, a customer value proposition, and an execution plan can be represented as shown in the following diagram:

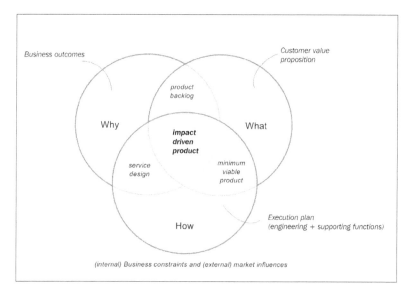

Case study

Throughout this book, we will use a sample business case to illustrate concepts. We will use an imaginary business called ArtGalore, which is an art gallery specializing in curating premium works of art. The company now wants to venture into creating a digital art viewing and purchasing experience for premium art buyers.

Let's look at the Lean Canvas model created for ArtGalore. The following is a sample representation:

2. PROBLEMS/ NEEDS	7. SOLUTION	3. UNIQUE VALUE PROPOSITION	9. UNFAIR ADVANTAGE	1A. EARLY ADOPTERS
Customers want to know about latest artworks, upcoming shows and get early access without having to visit gallery.	Online digital art gallery for buying art Smart recommendations social recommendations	Easily accessible, and delightful digital art buying experience that offers tastefully curated art collections, intuitive to the liking of our customers.	Expertise in curating art works Partnerships with renowned artists, and ability to source art works.	
Too expensive/ time consuming to reach out in time to customers with latest/ personalized collections	Prelaunch/ teasers of upcoming sale/ art catalog		Existing customer base, and artists	**1. CUSTOMER SEGMENTS** Premium art buyers
No easy way to find our what type of art our customers like	Double our revenues in the next 2 years Create a strong brand presence in premium art e-commerce.		**4. CHANNELS**	Art collectors
Unable to attract buyers beyond the physical retail location	Become the first choice of our target segment for buying art		Artists shows, online and offline galleries, corporate partnership	
2A. EXISTING ALTERNATIVES	**8. COSTS**	**6. REVENUES**		
Our competitors already have a digital experiance. There are many online art gallaries but our clientele's needs are mostly not met here	Warehousing Logistics partnerships Technology building costs Marketing Customer relationship	Continue sales through retail outlet Prebooking of art works on online channels		

In the preceding Lean Canvas model, the unique value proposition describes the concept of a digital art buying experience, the success metrics define the business goals, and the solution describes how the business intends to deliver the value proposition to its clientele. At the stage of problem/ solution fit, the actual execution plan of how this digital experience will be created is not yet finalized. Even the value proposition, target segment and solution are yet to be validated. The Lean Canvas model represents the big hypothesis that the business is making about its growth in the next two years. The Lean Canvas model, in a way, also represents a slightly longer-term view for the business. Along the way, as the business discovers more about the customer's perception of value and actual growth indicators, the canvas could change and ArtGalore could pivot to a different business model if the hypotheses are proven wrong.

From a product development perspective, we need to identify the three aspects of product success discussed earlier in this chapter.

Defining business outcomes that the product can deliver (why?)

What does the business hope to achieve by investing in a digital art gallery? The success metrics shown in the Lean Canvas model are a broad indicator of long-term goals. Building a brand and doubling revenue are long-term goals. In order to work toward those goals, the business needs to make some product investments in the short term.

Defining the value proposition that the product will create for the customer (what?)

The unique value proposition, and the solution concept, coupled with the customer segments, as described in the Lean Canvas model addresses this. It is natural for us to jump into ideas about product features, but before we even arrive at features, we need to think about user personas in our customer segment, and define how the solution will help to deliver the unique value proposition to them. Eventually, the features get refined into product functionality.

Defining the execution plan (how?)

There can be many ways to deliver the value proposition to the customer and to meet business outcomes. The execution plan for delivering the value proposition and business outcomes can depend on the ease of execution, cost of execution and, potential to create a positive impact on business outcomes. While the preferred solution for ArtGalore is a digital art gallery, not all aspects may need to be built in upfront. The execution plan must factor in the strengths of all the business functions that exist in ArtGalore. The focus must not be just about how technology can solve all customer problems/meet business outcomes. The focus must be about how to work seamlessly with business functions and ensure that the end-to-end product experience is satisfying.

Business constraints and market influence

Business constraints includes factors such as the time available to go to market and the potential to raise investments. Governing policies, regulations and compliances (if any), technology potential, capabilities, skills available, and so on can also influence business goals and the product experience. These factors will determine the key goals to focus on, the product features to offer, and the best way to implement them. In addition to constraints, the intrinsic business intent is important. What are our uncompromising principles? What do we value more? What values drive our decisions? What is our appetite for risk? These factors will decide how we deliver value.

A product can impact the business or the organization that is creating the product. It can also impact the customers who will adopt the product. An Impact Driven Product therefore is one that finds the best way to deliver value to customers and meet business outcomes under internal and external constraints.

Based on the unique value proposition and the business context and business outcomes prioritized for a specific time-bound milestone, the following is a sample illustration of the inputs for product development for ArtGalore:

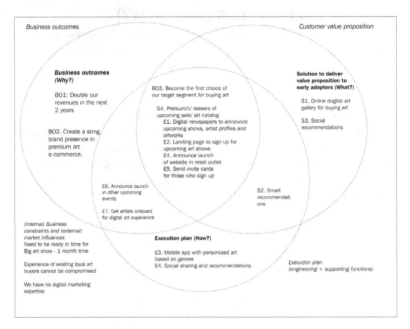

This is quite a simplified representation of the product development inputs at a given point in time. The diagram illustrates how business constraints may influence what the Impact Driven Product may deliver to the user.

The preceding illustration indicates that the most important outcome for ArtGalore is to become the first choice for art among its target segment. The most important aspect of the value proposition is offering tastefully curated art collections for existing buyers who don't have this information today. The most effective plan to execute this solution is to offer digital newsletters, provide an online sign-up for upcoming art shows, follow up on the sign-up with invites, and announce the website. This has been identified based on the business constraints of being ready for the upcoming art show, not compromising on the existing buyer experience, and so on. The other solutions, value propositions, and execution plans are also great, but given the business constraints, the Impact Driven Product is where we want to steer all our resources to.

Minimum Viable Product versus Impact Driven Product

Minimum Viable Product (**mvp**) is a concept that is quite prevalent in the software development scene. There are different interpretations of the concept of an mvp and *Chapter 6*, *Managing the Scope of an Impact Driven Product* dives into the interpretations of minimum viability.

At a basic level, an MVP intends to test the riskiest proposition of a business idea or a technology, without running out of resources. This is very helpful when testing an unproven technology or when building under tight business constraints. However, an mvp falls short in terms of delivering an end-to-end product experience to the consumers. The problem with how we define an mvp is that we tend to view technology viability as a value driver operating in isolation. An mvp is great in the problem/solution fit stage, but in the product/market fit stage, there are many other aspects to consider. When launching a new product, there are umpteen activities that need to be orchestrated to ensure success. Marketing, sales, support, and other operations need to come together to ensure a product's success. Testing viability of a product in isolation isn't going to ensure success for the business.

In my start-up, we had built up a platform for businesses to design and build mobile apps for client engagement. We had started out in the events and conferences domain, where app creation lead times were pretty low, audience engagement was critical, and last-minute changes to a schedule were quite common. Our platform was geared toward addressing those needs, but we soon started seeing interest from other business verticals who saw the potential that our platform had in driving customer engagement. One such business asked us to enhance our platform with the bespoke functionality.

We were in early stages in our start-up and naturally we got quite excited about the opportunity. The possibility of opening up our platform to another domain was quite lucrative. While we didn't see much value in creating a custom solution for a single client, we realized that we could enhance our platform to cater to the entire business vertical. This would also give us a great opportunity to launch our product into the B2C space. So, we carved out an mvp for this, and our engineers got busy with re-architecting the platform to make it flexible across business verticals. After spending more than a month on this, we were more or less ready with the revamped software.

Our revamped product was technologically viable. Yet, was the revamped software impact-driven? No. Why? We hadn't looked at the end-to-end value of the product. Our business model was different. Our target audience was new. A B2C market needed a very different approach. We hadn't planned for marketing, content creation, and promotions. We realized that we had neither the right skills nor the investment to drive this product to success. We hadn't really defined to ourselves what the new product would deliver. After all, we had just one customer who was interested. We hadn't looked at an end-to-end product experience.

Our rookie mistake cost us a month. We ended up shelving the product and didn't even close our sale with the one customer who showed interest. From the software perspective, we had it all covered, but we had not given any thought to the whole product experience or to the outcomes it could generate for our business. We are much better off today having learned and recovered from that mistake quickly, instead of having gone down that path, purely riding on the viability of our platform. We had looked at one customer's request and created a hypothesis about the problems our new platform could solve and the needs it could satisfy for that customer segment. We were confident that the product would address their needs and it could have. However, we hadn't given any thought about what it meant for our business, the stage we were in, our internal capabilities, and our weaknesses.

I know many developers who take great pride in how their software is built. The prevalent thinking is that if you build your software right, it will take care of itself. I've seen very smart engineers express deep disregard for supporting functions. They look down upon marketing, promotions, and sales saying, "People will adopt our product because my software is great." However, success isn't in and of the technology process itself. This is a core difference between task-oriented thinking and goal-oriented thinking.

Businesses make the same rookie mistake when going after early adopters. We want to get our business model validated quickly and cost-effectively. So, we build an mvp with a lot of loose ends on experience, revenue generation, and operations. Then we identify a safe pilot group from our family, friends, and well-wishers, or we offer our product for free to anyone who agrees to try it. Early adopters need to be potential (paying) customers who will risk adopting a product with partial experience, because it solves their most pressing needs. They will risk an incomplete product as long as their needs are met.

However, if we don't choose our early adopters right, we may end up validating the wrong product, which then tanks in the product/market fit stage. For instance, when we offer our product for free, how do we know if the customers are adopting our product because they see real value in it or because it's free? We feel happy with the validation we get for our software, but as we move out of that pilot group, we realize that our product doesn't have many takers. This is because we may have chosen our pilot group safely and they told us what we wanted to hear. The real test for a product is in testing out the riskiest propositions. The riskiest propositions are not just about how our product can create customer value, or about the technology viability in delivering that value, but also about the business capabilities.

If we're building a business, then we need to have a plan for how to make it grow, create impact, and be sustainable. Good software is never a replacement for a sound business model and vice versa. A product entering the product/market fit stage should have validated the viability of the riskiest business/technology propositions. Product/market fit should focus on offering an end-to-end product experience that offers the *most* value to the consumer and meets the business outcomes. The learnings that we have had right from product ideation and beyond have to continuously feed into the product experience. We need to think about a holistic product experience, rather than the feature set or technology.

If we don't realize that a product experience is a result of many technical and operational parts coming together, to meet a larger goal, then we're just missing the point. After all, we're not just laying the bricks; we're building a cathedral, a hospital, or a school.

An Impact Driven Product is the one that combines the technical and operational aspects of a product to create a holistic product experience. It comprises the entire product experience, across all touchpoints, for the customer. The Impact Driven Product ensures that we carve out a product, knowing full well what business outcomes to target. We factor in the support and co-ordination we need from business functions. We identify the smartest way to deliver value to customers under given business constraints. Knowing Key Business Outcomes is also a critical input to product development, and this should not be a one-time activity.

Key Business Outcomes

In early 2000, I worked as a business analyst. We were following the waterfall methodology, and I used to maintain huge 500-page requirements documents. Waterfall methodology assumes that software development happens in stages. The first phase is to understand business requirements. It is followed by designing and architecting the solution. Solution development starts only after the architecture is signed off testing begins only after development is complete, and so on.

Interactions with business stakeholders happened primarily at the requirements gathering phase. When building a large solution, that phase could run into months. There wasn't much interaction with businesses, or customers, after this phase. In my case, most of my interactions used to be confined to the analysis team. We used to be isolated from developers and testers. I mean, we actually sat on different floors, and in one instance, testers were in a different building altogether!

For the entire solution to be delivered, it could take many months, or even years. By then, a lot could have changed on the business scene. My first experience of understanding the impact of this came by chance. I was asked to fill in for my manager on a year-end prioritization call. I had to read out a one-line status update about a project we had been working on for six months at that point. I had no inkling about what the call was about. As a rather naïve junior analyst, I had no idea that all the regional business heads were going to be on the call. Toward the end of the two-hour long call, the facilitator read out a list of projects that were ongoing and in the pipeline for the next year. Every regional head made a go/no go decision, indicating whether they were willing to sponsor that project or not.

To my shock, an application that one of the teams had been building for two years got rejected. Poof! Just like that, two years of software development turned to ash. I was intrigued. How could this be? Why would they waste so much money building something and then scrap it on a whim? Was this only a problem with waterfall? How could we have anticipated business priorities?

I have witnessed many Agile projects shutting down not because we weren't building things right, but because the business context had changed. In some cases, the business ran out of money. Product teams were not closely aligned with business and while the business context had been shifting for a while, the previously identified backlog was still being built. In other cases, the product wasn't rolled out to users until much later, and adoption went downhill. Agility helps in responding to changing business context, but what if we could predict the trends of where the business is heading? The problem also occurs when business functions don't collaborate and work toward the same business outcomes. Even when the situation isn't calling for something as drastic as a shutdown, product teams are often taken by surprise about how a feature is perceived by a business. Business priorities need to align with every aspect of product building.

I know many a software engineer who is confounded by the idea of a quick-and-dirty working code, even when the code meets customer needs and business outcomes. I have seen business stakeholders fuss over the exact hue and shade of the brand colors in the user interface, and not really care so much about how performant the system is. Sometimes, this is due to an incorrect frame of reference. Some stakeholders don't really understand the effort that goes into optimizing a page load for an image-heavy website that is used by a million users. So, they may just brush it off and say, "Of course, that's to be expected. Why would it be otherwise?" This is because we make some assumptions about product outcomes. We treat a business outcome as a one-time requirement that is frozen for the lifetime of a product. We then iterate only on a product plan to deliver product features. We make assumptions about which customer value proposition is important. The business (as a whole) should determine trade-off decisions, the value proposition, and what customer feedback to act upon. Understanding business outcomes should also be iterative.

What value proposition do we need to deliver in our product? What business outcomes are we trying to meet? Isn't it wasteful for developers to build a highly performant system, when product differentiation is what we're going after? Isn't it just as wasteful for marketing teams to strategize about reach and engagement, when what we're really looking for are a few early adopters? These questions require collaboration and collective decision-making.

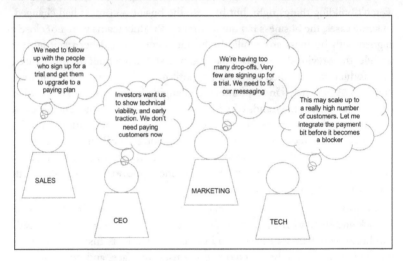

As shown in the preceding illustration, each of us holds a certain view of the business potential. Each of us is right in our own way. Brand messaging, sales follow-up, integrations to ease operational activities, and planning for scale are all good, but is it the right time now to address them? What determines this?

Where we direct our efforts depends on the present context of the business. This should not be a choice that business functions make in isolation. Business functions (product, marketing, sales operations, and so on) should collaboratively make this decision. Why we choose one way to execute over another, or what trade-offs we make, depends on the intrinsic organizational makeup. The combination of context and this choice determines business intent.

At every stage in a product's development (and especially at the start) we need to identify what drives the business intent. How do we plan on delivering the unique value proposition of our product to the customers/ market? What would tell us that we're doing the right thing for the business? What aspect of our value delivery is most important for us? What trade-offs are we making?

Growth, sustainability, and impact are pretty much the goals for every business (nonprofits and socio-political organizations may align better with impact than profitability). Yet if the business is not making money sustainably, or influencing sustainable change, can it exist? Should it exist? With this business goal, we can come up with a list of outcomes that are pertinent to the present business context. These outcomes can help us to align our product value propositions. They are the Key Business Outcomes we want to track. Each business outcome would have its own success metrics, which we can measure.

Some of these Key Business Outcomes are listed as follows. This list is indicative and generic. We may be able to identify other outcomes based on the context of our business. Typically, aim for not more than one to three outcomes:

- Growth
    ◦ Acquisitions (new registrations)
    ◦ Marketing (branding, reach, visibility, and virality)
    ◦ Scale (gearing up exponential growth)

- Sustainability
    ◦ Revenues (sales)
    ◦ Investments (fundraising)
    ◦ Costs (reduction/control)
    ◦ Streamlined operations (improved SLAs)

- Influence
    ◦ Retention (churn)
    ◦ Engagement (active users, support, and content)
    ◦ Adoption (training, access, and user experience)

As you may note, some of these outcomes are tangible and easily measurable, for instance, acquisitions. Others are quite abstract, such as customer satisfaction or marketing reach. In the next few chapters, we will try to define the criteria for measuring every business outcome.

Every business is unique and goes through different stages of maturity. Therefore, some business outcomes are likely to be more important than others, depending on which stage of business we are at, and what type of organization we are. Also, it's nearly impossible to go after everything listed earlier. We may spread ourselves too thinly trying to achieve success in every aspect. We will need to make trade-offs, and those trade-offs need to translate into the product.

The unique value proposition from our business model and the Key Business Outcomes form the basis for defining the Impact Driven Product. The following representation indicates the various steps in the Impact Driven Product development cycle:

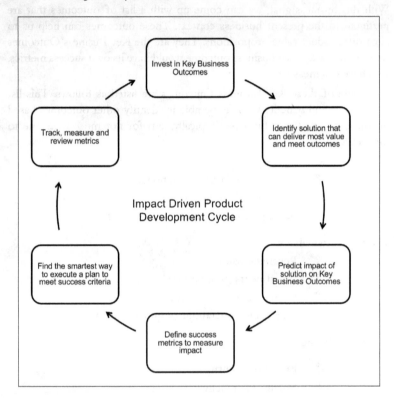

We will review each step in the Impact Driven Product cycle in the following chapters.

Summary

Practice trumps theory. While software methodologies and frameworks can guide us, our interpretation and adoption of these frameworks in our unique context matters a lot. The focus needs to remain on measuring outcomes and not the output. Product development needs to factor in business outcomes, customer value, an execution plan, and internal and external constraints to ensure that a holistic end-to-end product experience can be created. Identifying the Key Business Outcomes is an important input to product development, and this should not be a one-time activity. Being cognizant of the business constraints, and staying aligned on Key Business Outcomes, can ensure that we don't lose focus of the metrics that will make our business succeed.

Identifying Key Business Outcomes is the first step towards getting the organization aligned on goals. In the next chapter we will find out about why and how we can invest in these outcomes.

2

INVEST IN KEY BUSINESS OUTCOMES

In the previous chapter, we defined our business model and identified Key Business Outcomes. However, this cannot be a one-time activity. We need to continually evaluate and invest in the outcomes that matter. Responding to change is not the onus of just product development. Agility in business decisions is equally important. Product development must work in conjunction with these business decisions and every business function must be aligned to the changes that the business is responding to.

Accordingly, this chapter will address the following queries:

- How can product development include business agility as part of the development cycle?
- How to play the Investment Game and capture the value for each Key Business Outcome?

Investments

The best time to plant a tree was 20 years ago. The second best time is now.
— Chinese proverb

Planning for success in life generally involves making investment decisions. We must decide how to invest our time, which people to invest in, where to invest our money, and so on. We need to start some investments today to reap the benefits a year, or even 20 years, from now. Some investments return immediate benefits, such as winning a game or preparing for an interview to get into a job. Some investments need much longer time, but spreading out an investment could make it last a lifetime.

Trudging through school, for instance, will eventually pay off. Some investments burn your money, and create no monetary value, but they bring a lot of joy. These could be a nice vacation, buying a car, or throwing a party. When we don't understand what benefits we should be reaping from an investment, we tend to have unrealistic expectations. We also need to be realistic about how long it will take for an investment to return benefits. Needless to say, everything comes with its own risks.

Building products is no different. Some features take a long time to build and will return investment in the long term. Some features give immediate benefits. Building products without understanding business benefits is wasteful and expensive?. This is why we start with identifying the Key Business Outcomes for our product. Product building depends on available talent, capital, and other operating constraints. So, if we have unlimited time, money, and favorable conditions, then yes, we can build anything, but that never happens. Product building, like everything else in life, operates under constraints.

We need to identify, as a business, where to focus our efforts and capital. We also need to set realistic expectations about benefits and timelines. We must know how our past investments have performed. This information will help us plan our product funnel.

Time-bound priorities for Key Business Outcomes

To create the best product experience, we must align product-building and business operations. To do this, we need to find the most important (one to three) business outcomes for a definite timeline. The reason I'm saying one to three outcomes is because in early stages of product development, it is best to steer our resources toward fewer outcomes. Going after too many goals can be counter-productive and can result in a loss of focus.

Quoting *Eric Ries*, author of *The Lean Startup*, here:

> *"There is no reason why a product cannot have both high margins and high retention. However, in my experience, successful startups focus on just one engine of growth, specializing in everything that is required to make it work."*

Even when we focus only on growth, sustainability, or influence as our high-level goals, we may still need to refine to one to three outcomes within these high-level goals, to ensure that we direct our efforts constructively. Based on the Key Business Outcomes, we can determine which product functionality to pursue and which functionalities are likely to be the most impactful.

Setting a time limit helps us to define realistic product backlogs. We can then track success metrics and evaluate whether or not the product is working/successful. This is typically the time needed to execute a plan and start seeing results. We need to be able to assess whether the product is meeting desired goals or not. An indefinite timeline may lead to overengineering. Why? Let me recount an experience from a software engineer who left his day job to start up a business in online music streaming. He had started with a great idea and immense passion. When I met him, he told me that he had been working on his product for a year.

When I asked him how many users had signed up, he said, "None!" I was quite curious to know why this was the case. When I probed further, he explained that he wanted his product to be perfect. He kept adding tweaks and subtleties, trying to make his product good enough to be showcased to the world. He hadn't set himself a time-bound goal, nor a milestone so that he could meet specific goals. He kept pursuing *perfection*, and this pursuit was limited to his choice of features (functionalities) in the product. His pursuit of perfection in how the product was being built was not supported by an equal zeal to meet any outcomes. He hadn't thought of how many users he wanted to acquire, whether he wanted to make revenues from his product or not, or what users might want in the product. He was running out of money in about three months and was desperate to find takers for his product. He hadn't laid the groundwork for anything other than the functional aspects of the product. He had been running on an indefinite timeline and overengineering a product that had neither users nor a business model.

Ash Maurya, in his book *Running Lean*, describes the three stages of a start-up:

- Problem /solution fit
- Product /market fit
- Scale

The development of a product follows the same stages. The problem /solution phase must be less about product development, and more about validating the unique value proposition.

Once we have validated the unique value proposition, we have a clear idea of what the product is, who our customers are, what alternatives we trying to replace, and so on. This is the phase where we're trying to see if our product meets the needs of our customers. Product /market fit is the stage where we figure out if our product can meet the market's needs. Does the market see value in our product? If yes, then how do customers value our product? How does that translate into a business outcome for us? The third stage of scale happens after we have established the product /market fit and have found a business model that is repeatable, and the quest is to accelerate growth.

The Impact Driven Product, as we saw in *Chapter 1*, *Identify Key Business Outcomes,* is a combination of the why, what, and how under the influence of internal and external factors. An Impact Driven Product, therefore, is one that finds the best way to deliver value to customers and meet business outcomes under internal and external constraints.

During the problem/solution fit and the product/market fit stages, we define the product, measure its success, and iterate on our learnings. It is important that we keep the build-measure-learn loop short. It must be short enough to ensure that we don't overengineer our product and long enough to be able to deliver something of value.

Typically, a few weeks to a one or two-month period can work well when we're in these early stages of product development. It helps us to keep our validation cycle shorter and keep our focus on identifying our Impact Driven Product. As our product matures (gains traction), we start seeing evidence of success in business outcomes. We then decrease the frequency of this validation cycle or increase the duration of the validation cycle. We could extend the frequency of investing in Key Business Outcomes to four to six months, depending on the nature and maturity of the product.

There is of course the question of what if we cannot implement an idea in three months? What if we don't have the right skills, or the resources, to meet the business outcomes? We still need to understand realistic implementation and validation timelines. This is what we will establish in later stages in the development cycle described in the next two chapters.

Trade-offs in time-bound planning

When implementing software, there will be trade-offs that we need to make. The product trade-offs might be about speed, quality, performance, reliability, or scalability. Typically, we categorize them under nonfunctional requirements. Some get classified as technical tasks and never make it onto the radar of nontechnical folks. This is where most of the disconnect between the technical and nontechnical teams arises.

When we're in the early stages of product development, we tend to have a narrow product focus. We target a limited set of early adopters. We may also look at a limited feature set. One of the main reasons we want to do this is to iterate through the build-measure-learn loop swiftly. We want to validate our product assumptions at the earliest opportunity, so sometimes the quick-and-dirty code may just work. The problem here is that the product could have defects. It might not work well for all use cases, it might not scale or be very responsive, and so on. Yet these trade-offs are being made at the product engineering level. Without understanding what measurable outcomes that we seek from the product at this stage, we cannot make educated trade-off decisions.

For instance, what is our idea of early adopters? How many users are we targeting? If a product works well for the early adopters, how soon do we want to scale to the next level? What if we started with 50 customers, and now we have 200 sign-ups? What trade-off is the business willing to make? Is it OK if we lose customers because of limiting performance or defects? Should product teams decide this in isolation? Don't other business functions have a stake/say in this?

When making trade-off decisions in isolation, technical teams build defensive code. They are unclear about success metrics. They assume that the business will come back with more sales, so they build less features, but more robust software. Nontechnical folks, when making trade-off decisions may do so with a poor frame of reference about technology. Evaluating the benefits of the effort involved in building quick-and-dirty software versus robust scalable software, can be hard. The end result of this disconnect is the loss of experience for customers and the loss of value to a business.

In some cases, there may be immediate benefits. Defining the timelines for realizing product benefits in terms of actionable metrics is required to define what to build now and what not to build now.

Investing in Key Business Outcomes

The following representation shows the stages of product development for creating our Impact Driven Product:

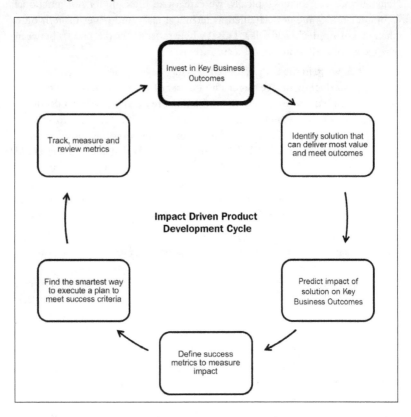

We have initiated our first step in the product development. This first step is **Invest in Key Business Outcomes**. At this stage, the business indicates an inclination to build a solution that will impact certain business outcomes. Now, we may be able to build some functionality in this solution faster and therefore we can meet outcomes sooner. Some other functionality may take longer to build and may take a longer time to meet outcomes. We may have to make conscious technology and experience trade-offs to meet time-bound priorities.

So how do we know which trade-offs are worth making?

As we iterate through the build-measure-learn loop of the product, it is likely that we will discover customer insights, feedback, gaps in product experience, and so on.

How do we decide which learning, feedback, or customer insight is important?

Product teams should not answer this question in isolation. Since a product's success influences business outcomes (and vice versa), it is important to understand what risks, trade-offs, and goals the business is willing to consider. These decisions influence how business functions and product development should spend their resources. We could, of course, ask for different priorities on a case-by-case basis. However, it will be ineffective to look at a bunch of disparate data, insights from live functionality, and a backlog of potential functionality and then prioritize without context.

This is same comparison that *Jeff Paton* uses when describing how user stories are managed in a product backlog. The preceding image illustrates this perspective. He says, "We spend lots of time working with our customers. We work hard to understand their goals, their users, and the major parts of the system we could build. Then we finally get down to the details – the pieces of functionality we'd like to build... after all that work, after establishing all that shared understanding I feel like we pull all the leaves off the tree and load them into a leaf bag – then cut down the tree. That's what a flat backlog is to me. A bag of context-free mulch." (`https://jpattonassociates.com/the-new-backlog/`)

This is exactly what happens when we draw up a business model, then forget about the business drivers, and execute a product plan focused only on the product backlog. So, when business stakeholders are asked to prioritize a backlog without context, we can't expect to get the inputs we seek. Also, this type of prioritization (which essentially indicates the value (or ranking) that a business attaches to a product functionality or to a customer experience) cannot be quantified. Prioritization also needs to start with Key Business Outcomes and the business constraints that determine product strategy. Key Business Outcomes must be measurable.

In order to assign a value/rank to the business drivers, we need to understand what significance the business attaches to it. Instead of this being a random number or something we rank on a scale of one to ten, we can match it closely to how the business actually operates. Businesses make bets on outcomes. Each bet comes with its risk and will take a certain amount of time to reap benefits. When planning personal financial investments, to make a comparison, we're likely to plan based on our risk appetite and financial goals. This is similar to predicting a certain rate of interest/growth on our investments, at a certain time in future. Just asking business stakeholders about their investment priorities doesn't usually help, so I recommend that we play an Investment Game!

Playing the Investment Game—what outcomes will the business bet on in the next one-to-two months?

The Investment Game needs to be played as a collaborative exercise with representation from all stakeholders. A stakeholder is one of these:

- Anyone who is likely to influence product decisions
- Anyone who is impacted by product outcomes
- Anyone who is involved in product implementation

Buy a Feature game

The Investment Game draws inspiration from the Buy a Feature game. If you have played Buy a Feature (`http://www.innovationgames. com/buy-a-feature/`), then you may be familiar with the format of this game. The idea of the game is to help stakeholders to get a sense of how costly a product feature is. The trigger for getting stakeholders to "buy a feature" is when we have a product backlog that has been estimated by developers, and we know that within the give time/budget we may be unable to deliver the backlog. The Buy a Feature game is an effective way of asking stakeholders to indicate feature priorities. It is also quite effective when asking stakeholders to indicate "must haves" and "should haves" on the product backlog.

The cost for each feature is determined on roughly sizing the feature cost in terms of the effort needed to build it. The game is very practical and has a dramatic influence on how business stakeholders view features. It's like stakeholders are shopping for features with limited money, and that brings in a real-world view of operating under financial constraints.

The Investment Game is different in that it does not require costs to be derived upfront. It is essentially following the format of using real money and using a limited amount of money, but that's where the similarity with the Buy a Feature game ends.

This is what we need for playing the Investment Game:

1. A list of Key Business Outcomes

2. Data (market trends, customer insights, feedback, and success metrics) that can influence business decisions

3. Limited amount of real money (capital to invest)

What we don't need for playing the Investment Game is this:

1. Product functionality/features/backlog items

2. Costs

We limit the amount of capital that is allowed to be invested. While it may be possible to raise money for the business, the reality is that product building does operate under constraints. Limiting the money available to play this game helps us to artificially enforce that constraint and forces people to critically evaluate their choices. We are not concerned about the costs or actual product functionality for playing this game. This is an iteration on the business model thinking and an attempt to capture the risk and investment appetite of the business.

We ask stakeholders to plan their investment priorities, by indicating how much money they are willing to invest on delivering a solution (the Impact Driven Product) that meets a business outcome. At this point, we're not yet defining how the product will contribute to that value, or how to measure the benefits from this investment. We will do that in the next step in the Impact Driven Product development cycle.

During the early stages of product development, we may or may not have many data points to back up our decisions. If the product has not yet been launched, then insights from problem interviews with customers can feed into this activity. Typically, we may invest in outcomes that correspond to our product's core value propositions or those that validate our riskiest propositions. Also, since this is a collaborative activity, it forces stakeholders to actively discuss and debate their investments. This can quickly get into a war of opinions, and it is best kept in check by presenting any data available.

> *"If we have data, let's look at data. If all we have are opinions, let's go with mine."*
> *– Jim Barksdale, Netscape*

An organization's culture has a big role to play in the effectiveness of this exercise. In a culture that fosters collaboration, diversity of ideas, data-backed decision-making, and decentralized teams, there is a higher chance to garner better outcomes from this activity.

Let's look at our list of business outcomes again:

* Growth
    ○ Acquisitions (new registrations)
    ○ Marketing (branding, reach, visibility, and virality)
    ○ Scale (gearing up exponential growth)

- Sustainability
    - ° Revenues (sales)
    - ° Investments (fundraising)
    - ° Costs (reduction/control)
    - ° Streamlined operations (improved SLAs)

- Influence
    - ° Retention (churn)
    - ° Engagement (active users, support, and content)
    - ° Adoption (training, access, and user experience)

Let's consider this is the initiation of product development for the ArtGalore digital gallery, introduced in *Chapter 1*, *Identify Key Business Outcomes*. We have our business model (Lean Canvas). We also have insights from problem interviews with customers. We are ready to determine what solution to build in order to meet the business constraints of launching this before the Big Art Show (refer to the business outcomes, business context and constraints, and market factors in the following image). We have a high-level idea of the solution from the Lean Canvas model.

The question we're trying to answer here is: what business outcome should we try to meet within the one-month timeline dictated by the business/market constraint? Should we look at brand building? Should we look at revenues?

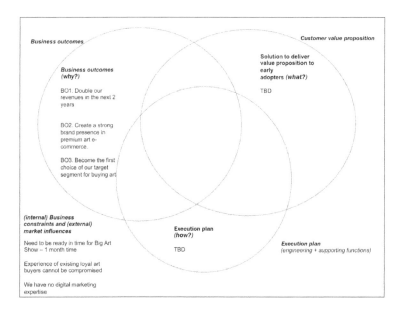

As you may observe, the one-month timeline is only to launch the solution. It is not a timeline for creating a brand presence or making revenue. Those will come into effect only after the solution is launched. However, given the time constraints our lack of digital marketing expertise, and based on insights we have from problem interviews and existing customers, and so on, the business needs to decide which business outcome to invest in.

From the list of business outcomes under growth, sustainability, and influence, we may determine that acquisitions, revenue, engagement, and marketing, all seem to be geared toward doubling the revenue in two years. Among these, is there a relative priority? Each stakeholder could have a different perspective of what we need to invest in, based on what we know today. They also need to gauge relative priorities between these outcomes. As in, how valuable is getting a good number of qualified leads (marketing)? Is it more valuable than converting these leads into registered users (acquisitions)? Is that less valuable than getting customers to pay (revenues)? However, since the amount of money to play the Investment Game is limited, they will have to carefully choose where they want to invest.

So, let's say that the stakeholders collectively determine that they want to invest in engagement (of existing customers) and revenue. Now, this decision is based on the people and the unique context of the business. No two businesses are alike, and hence the choice of where they want to invest may be different:

- Business #1 may invest as shown in the following figure:

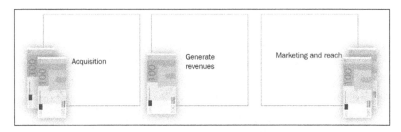

- Business #2 may invest as shown in the following figure:

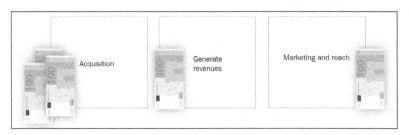

The ArtGalore business may choose to invest as shown in the following figure:

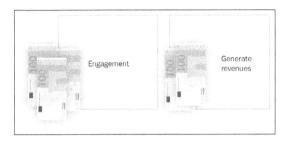

There is no right or wrong way to make an investment, but this nature of input allows the product team to focus on building a solution that is driven by business context. It is indeed possible that a decision could backfire. It is also possible that a business may lose customers due to poor user experience. That is the risk that the business is willing to take when stakeholders indicate their preference.

In a product that is already being used, we are likely to have insights from customers. We may have data on engagement, adoption, revenue, reach, and so on. This is also the right forum to highlight our critical metrics and see if that influences business inclination to invest. For instance, customer support could highlight the rise in customer complaints due to a feature that we recently launched. The stakeholders may consider this data, but they might feel that it does not impact our primary goals of revenue and growth. This also means that the business is willingly making a trade-off by prioritizing revenue over adoption.

The important thing at this stage is to enable conversations between stakeholders. This activity helps the stakeholders to pitch to each other what business outcome they feel is critical. It gives them an opportunity to evaluate their priorities as a group. It is worthwhile spending as much time as needed having discussions, especially when there are conflicting points of view. This is also the main reason for ensuring that all stakeholders participate in this activity, since it allows them to get a sense of the overall priorities and provides a forum for pitching the priorities of their individual business functions.

When I ran this activity in a nonprofit, there were about seven stakeholders who participated. In the lead-up before the session, I had individual conversations with many business stakeholders. I listened to a lot of passionate ideas about influencing the community they were trying to serve. I also listened to a lot of ideas that floated around the visibility of their brand and how to increase their reach. It was noteworthy that the engineering team had a different mandate altogether. They had been working on performance fixes and automating operation tasks! Eventually, when the group got together, fundraising for the organization came out as their top priority. Nearly no money was invested in marketing, community impact, or operational efficiency!

This was the first time that the group got together to discuss and review their priorities. They could establish that the lack of visibility surrounding funding was their biggest bottleneck in delivering impact. Unless they raised funds, they would be unable to reach any of their milestones that were planned for later that year. While there were other areas that needed attention, the group agreed that fundraising needed the most attention. This then set the tone of product development. Product managers should ideally be a key stakeholder in this type of activity and also facilitate this activity since the output from the activity feeds into product priorities.

The final output from the Investment Game captures the business outcomes that were prioritized (for a specific timeline) and the amount invested against each of them. These values will be used in the subsequent prioritization of product functionality/value proposition and trade-offs.

The following table captures the amount that, in our example, ArtGalore stakeholders invested in their Key Business Outcomes. We now have a value for the most important business outcomes.

Business outcome →	Engagement	Generate revenue
Invested amount →	300	200

At the end of one month, once we have launched our first version of the product experience, we need to get all the stakeholders back together to review any other insights we have and determine the next milestone. Once again, we will evaluate the business context and the investment that we are making in Key Business Outcomes. For instance, it is possible that either our competitor beat us to the market, we raised new investments, or we signed up a celebrity artist since the last time we evaluated our business context. These factors can influence how we want to steer our product and our investment decisions.

Iterating through business priorities in the language they speak is important when we're setting the stage for product development. It can help to guide product development in a tangible, measureable, and iterative model. This also helps us to avoid surprises later, as we proactively think about where the business is headed to and make an implementation plan that can align with the business direction, while still delivering maximum value to customers. Being proactive in identifying and investing in Key Business Outcomes can help us to avoid situations where we have built a product that is no longer useful for the business.

Summary

In this chapter, we learned that we need to know what to build when iterating through the build-measure-learn loop. Determining what to build cannot be an isolated decision made by the product teams. The direction on product strategy needs to be based on the Key Business Outcomes. Investments made provide us with a way to measure the value that a business places on Key Business Outcomes. Doing this in shorter focused iterations, with insights from the market, product metrics, and the current business context and constraints, enables us to make informed decisions and respond effectively to changing trends.

In the next chapter, we will figure out what solution to build in order to deliver the most value to customers and what the best way is to meet business outcomes.

3

IDENTIFY THE SOLUTION AND ITS IMPACT ON KEY BUSINESS OUTCOMES

Ideation is a wonderfully creative process that can help us to take leaps into solutions. When building products under ambiguous conditions, we don't know how customers will adopt our product, how to deliver the best experience, or even which problems are more important to solve. Ideas can help us to navigate ambiguity by throwing open possibilities that we couldn't see earlier. At the same time, ideas can distract us from our goals. Product managers must be able to take ideas in their stride and be able to differentiate between ideas that add value and those that sound important but create no value. However, this does not have to be an individual's judgment. This happens best when we collaborate with business functions and stakeholders to estimate the impact and ensure that we share the same definition of success. This chapter proposes a framework for evaluating the impact of ideas on Key Business Outcomes.

The framework will ensure that we carry over only the most impactful feature ideas into the product backlog. Our backlog can then be lean, and we can focus all our resources on delivering the most value both to the customer and to the business.

In this regard, this chapter addresses the following points, describing how to do these:

- Finding the right problem to solve
- Creating an end-to-end view of the user and business (product/service) interaction
- Identifying feature ideas
- Estimating impact on Key Business Outcomes and derive value scores
- Prioritizing feature ideas based on value scores

Finding the right problem to solve

> *"An idea is like a virus. Resilient. Highly contagious. And even the smallest seed of an idea can grow. It can grow to define or destroy you."*
> - Cobb, Inception

A friend recently observed that any conversation in Bengaluru (India) sooner or later steers toward traffic woes. Invariably, everyone claims to have a solution for Bengaluru's traffic woes. You get to hear all sorts of ideas: fix all the potholes, build flyovers, introduce more public transport, and get those hyperloops or even flying cars. There are so many ideas, but our traffic woes persist.

We are creatures of imagination and ideas. We love fantasy. We dream up a reality that doesn't exist today, but that is also our biggest strength. Ideas can motivate us to strive for the impossible, but that is also the bane of ideas. There is a very fuzzy line between difficult and impossible. We end up chasing our tails trying to pursue ideas that sound important. Why is that? Is it because we don't understand our problem well enough? If we don't know what problem we're solving, how can we find the right solution?

In many cases, the problem is ubiquitous, for instance, the Bengaluru traffic problem. You only need to drive on Bengaluru roads twice to come up with a laundry list of issues. The traffic problem is real, unique, and personal to each of us. So, of course, everyone has a solution. Just because everyone has an idea, it doesn't mean those solutions are viable and valuable. Some ideas just aren't practical. Some ideas need way more investment. Some ideas are culturally bound to fail and some won't even take off because of political or social reasons. Some ideas will take a really long time before they start making a difference. Meanwhile, we find our own little ways to circumvent the problem. We work from home, take the bus, drive in off-peak hours, carpool, work in shifts, move closer to workplaces, take de-stressing yoga classes, and so on.

When we know enough about the problem, it is more valuable, effective, and fun to ideate. People love to ideate even about seemingly hard-to-solve problems. Sometimes, viability or the lack of viability of a solution can help us understand the problem better. When operating under uncertainty (where we are yet to fully grasp the potential of the market or what our customers value), we need to make ideas our friends. Finding ideas for a product isn't the hardest part, because ideas come cheap. The hard part is always finding the idea that will deliver our unique value proposition and business outcomes. By the way, ideas often come disguised as implementation specifics. So, product management also has to deal with sorting out the "how" from the "what."

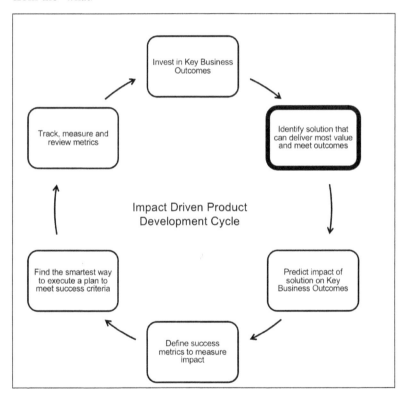

To build or not to build?

During the first few months at my start-up, we built an early version of an event app platform to engage conference audiences. We sold our product to a few conference organizers. One of our ideas was that event organizers would love the ability to make changes to schedules on the fly and they would want to notify the attendees about these changes. We had two parts to our solution: an admin console that could be used only from a laptop and an end user-facing mobile app. The problem was that our customers (the event organizer) wanted only a well-designed, visually-appealing, and white-labeled app. They were willing to pay us only for the solution that would amplify the value they were providing to their customers. The event organizers rarely used the admin console. They sought our help whenever they needed to use any functionality in the admin console.

When we sat down as a team, we observed with dismay that the organizers never or rarely used real-time notifications. We jumped to the conclusion that they were not using them because they were accessible on a laptop and not on their mobile phones. I remember we spent three hours having a heated debate about the best way to solve this. We wanted our platform to be a DIY platform. We came up three ideas: building a mobile admin console, creating a WhatsApp-like chat, or notifying the attendees using SMS. All our ideas were based on two big assumptions:

1. Our customers needed real-time notifications

2. They needed to send notifications from their mobile phones

After our three hours of healthy discussion in our start-up team, we realized that none of our customers had complained about not being able to send notifications to attendees themselves so far. We didn't know if it was because they didn't know about the feature or they didn't use it because it was available only on the desktop admin console. We, once again, jumped to the conclusion that the customers actually needed the ability to send notifications but weren't complaining. So far, our customers had always called us a day before the event and relied on us to make the necessary changes from the admin console. So, we threw open more ideas to somehow build this into the product so that it could become a DIY (Do-It-Yourself) value proposition. We could never reach a consensus on what that solution would look like. There was other functionality that customers were asking for, and we had limited resources. So, we decided to wait it out, while gathering data, observing, and talking to our customers, before we decided on an approach. In retrospect, this was one of the smartest things we did.

Over the following eight months, we had one or two occasions where conference organizers wanted the ability to send notifications themselves. They told us that they couldn't bring a laptop to the venue. On those occasions, we charged them extra, and sent in an intern and a laptop to help during the event. We eventually built the feature enabling notifications for more than a year, and 40 conferences, later. We built it mainly to reduce our operational costs rather than as a benefit to the customer. It was not sustainable to send an intern and a laptop anymore. So, the feature was built in with an unpolished UI and with just enough functionality that we had seen used in the past year. All along, event organizers had expected us to support them with last-minute schedule changes.

We thought that by making it easier for our customers to send notifications and the feature accessible on mobile we could increase our revenue, because event organizers would be willing to pay more for a DIY feature. While they were willing to pay more for the functionality (of making real-time changes), they weren't really keen on the DIY aspect. If anything, it added more to their workload, and they were extremely stretched and the time constrained during the days of the event already.

We realized that this feature was not a revenue generator, but a cost saver. Since the organizers were always leaning on us to help with last-minute changes, we had to find the best way to optimize our costs and time in responding to their requests. We would have had to take a very different approach had we wanted to turn this into a revenue generator, and that could have been an undertaking that we as a team may have been unprepared for.

There was nothing wrong with the ideas that we had. What we didn't know was the impact our ideas could deliver. A reflective pause is essential between an idea and finding the best way to implement the idea. The reflective pause should help us to understand our users. It should also help us to understand what we would gain as a business from our idea and make it possible to define and plan for the success of your idea.

Often, we tend to look at the product features in isolation. We prioritize features based on relative merit, rarely questioning if a feature is needed at all. In the case of my start-up, we could have made the mistake of evaluating if SMS notifications were more valuable than the mobile admin console. However, the more important questions were: do we need this feature? Is there a better way to deliver the value proposition without building anything more than what we already have? Should we instead build something else more valuable? For us, customer acquisitions and conversions were the most important business outcomes. One way we could have validated the value of this feature was by explicitly creating pricing plans, which excluded/included the notification feature and validated if it impacted our acquisitions. We could then have asked: are our leads converting because we have this feature? Are our customers opting for the plan that includes notifications? We hadn't been very smart about this, but at least we learned an important lesson! Prioritizing features requires finding that fine intersection between "why," "what," and "how." Let's begin with identifying the product features.

Creating an end-to-end view of the user and business (product/service) interaction

To understand customers' pain points, needs, and their user journeys, we need to have a good grasp of the user personas in our target segment. We also need to be able to map each persona's journey into the product functionality.

User story maps are an effective way to organize user activities and to model the functionality of an application. They are valuable in identifying product features from a user's perspective, and are a great tool for visualizing and planning product releases. Service design thinking helps us to think through how a service can be delivered to meet a user's needs. It enables us to think through all the touch points and interactions with our users, helping us to identify bottlenecks, dependencies, and delays.

The following are some of the principles of service design (https://www.interaction-design.org/literature/article/the-principles-of-service-design-thinking-building-better-services):

- Services should be designed based on customer needs rather than the internal needs of the business

- Services should be designed to deliver a unified and efficient system rather than component-by-component, which can lead to poor overall service performance
- Services should be designed based on creating value for users and customers and to be as efficient as possible

When identifying product features, it's valuable to leverage both story maps and service design. It gives us a holistic view of user interactions, and touchpoints, instead of just isolated product features. I usually blend in service touchpoints with story maps, because it helps me to identify triggers for user actions and view offline user actions in the overall context of how a user interacts with our product.

For instance, when we think about first-time users, it helps to think through how a user would discover our product. We can then blend in supporting operational touchpoints and think about our product holistically. It also helps us to differentiate hygiene functionalities from value adds, for instance, login/authentication. Login by itself adds no value to anyone. A user does not gain any benefit by logging in to an app. Login doesn't sell, unless you're building an authentication service. Yet we need to build a login feature nevertheless, because it is a necessary functionality.

Login makes sense only in the context of defining what meets a user's goals: making features accessible based on user credentials. Then, it is important to identify how a guest user will use our product, compared to a logged in user. Login just becomes a small detail in an end-to-end product experience. It also helps us to think about the user's context when using the feature. Will the user access our app from the comfort of their home, or are they on the road when using our app? Is there connectivity? These questions can have a bearing on how we design the functionality.

There is a big difference in perspective between task-oriented thinking and goal-oriented thinking. Jeff Patton's *User Story Mapping – User Story Mapping, Discover the Whole Story, Build the Right Product* (also descried in *Chapter 2, Invest in Key Business Outcomes*) is a great tool for keeping our focus on a user's goals without getting distracted by the application's features. I was fortunate enough to attend one of Jeff's workshops on user story mapping many years ago. It was one of the most valuable leaps in product thinking for me. At that time, the prevalent way of product backlog and scope management was still a very system-centric view, but user story mapping showed how effective it can be when we visualize the product backlog and align it with a user's context. It changed the way I thought about prioritization and scope management.

The following is a sample story map for the digital art gallery case study introduced in **Chapter 1**, *Identify Key Business Outcomes*. It represents a part of the story map for the premium art buyers. The flow captures the need of customers to get early access and stay tuned to upcoming artworks and art shows:

User	Premium art buyers							
Goals	I want to get early access to upcoming art shows, artworks so that I can stay up-to-date, and make early decision on my art purchases							
Activities	Subscribe to newsletter in under 30 seconds on mobile or desktop			Receive newsletter		Unsubscribe		
Sub Activities	Sign up on website	Sign up by calling relationship manager/ customer support	Sign up by email	Get by email	Get by postal mail	Opt out on website	Opt out by email/calling

In the preceding story map, there are subactivities that are not necessarily in the online product. For instance, "sign up by calling relationship manager/customer support" is not something that the product engineering team is required to build. This step may instead be implemented by the supporting functions. Yet this option for users to sign up by calling the relationship manager is an important aspect to capture on the story map. I've extended service design aspects into the story mapping itself. This presents a complete view of our product experience, rather than just a technology product's focus.

While the preceding story map captures the activities from a customer perspective, we also need to capture what happens internally to meet this customer need. The marketing team, customer relationship team, art curators, and customer support, all have a part to play in ensuring that this customer goal is met. The following is a sample story map for the marketing team:

User	Marketing team							
Goals	I want to present content about the best artworks, artists and upcoming shows so as to increase customer engagement							
Activities	Collect details for content in newsletter		Prepare newsletter template		Put together content in newsletter format		Send newsletter to all signed up subscribers	
Sub Activities	Collaborate with artists	Collaborate with art curation team	Create offline brochure template	Create online brochure template	Prepare pictures and text copy	Proofread and edit content	Get list of subscribers	Sent newsletter

A huge advantage of thinking through all possible interactions that a user can have with our business (product and service) early on is that it gives us alternative options for delivering a user's goal. It opens up our thinking about how we can deliver value to the user, while meeting our business outcomes, and ensuring that we don't run out of resources. This helps us to stay lean. At different stages of product maturity, we may have a task-level breakdown for subactivities. Yet, we could evaluate priorities at an activity level. This gives us the freedom to then negotiate how best to deliver value for that activity, without being bound to task-level details.

Typically, product engineering teams use MoSCoW prioritization (must haves, should haves, nice to haves, and won't have; refer to `https://www.agilebusiness.org/content/moscow-prioritisation-0`). Buy a Feature games also help in product feature prioritization, and 2×2 cost value matrices are another great way to visualize product priorities. While all of these methods seem perfectly fine in theory, there are some pitfalls when using them.

Jeff Patton compares a flat product backlog to looking at a bag of leaves instead of seeing leaves as part of the whole tree. When features/stories are presented for prioritization to stakeholders without the user context, it is hard to understand what loss of experience might occur due to their prioritization decisions. Feature A may seem like a 'nice to have' to the business, but it may be very valuable to the user. Feature B may seem like a 'must have' for the business, but it might not be easily supported, and hence might not give the user much value. A flat backlog doesn't offer this context.

Another pitfall is prioritization based on cost/effort. The need to manage scope arises out of an inability to meet timelines and budgets, based on our estimates of costs, complexity, and effort. Even if feature A costs more than feature B, it may be able to drive a much higher value to customers or bring about better business outcomes. Cost alone cannot determine priorities.

In order to increase the context for prioritizing product functionality, we need to understand its impact in terms of the following:

- The features that increase value to customers
- How a user feature impacts Key Business Outcomes

In my start-up, real-time changes and notifications were valuable to customers only when they had a support team that could handle these changes. DIY was not practical for them, since it only increased the workload for an already overworked team that was hard-pressed for time. It did nothing to increase our KBO of increasing revenues and acquisitions. So, it was right to not have tried to perfect or improvise on the basic functionality that we already had. However, later, when we had too many requests from our customers and when we had more events happening on the same day, it was hard to sustain costs when supporting these events. We needed the feature to be improvised to meet our needs to help us to support customer needs without burning out. Our KBO had shifted to sustain operations for a certain period of time.

Estimating impact on Key Business Outcomes and derive value scores

Once we have a backlog of user features, we need to estimate the impact of those features on invested business outcomes. I use the word "estimate," since we're only trying to guess the extent of the impact that a feature could have on our business outcomes. Even when we have data and insights about usage patterns and needs, we may not be able to accurately pinpoint our product's performance. Since businesses (and products) operate under high ambiguity, we may have little control over what could influence our product's performance. So, in order for us to plan ahead, we have to rely on past data, our business aspirations, our resources, our capabilities, our strengths, and our weaknesses:

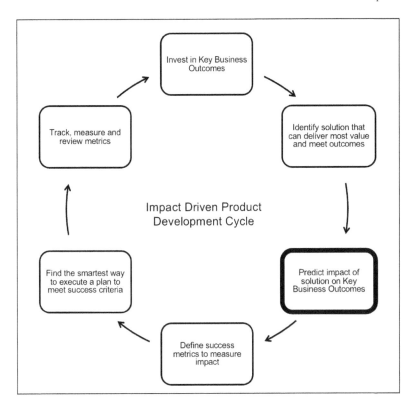

Deriving value scores

In *Chapter 2, Invest in Key Business Outcomes*, we discussed using the Investment Game. We were able to capture the amount that business stakeholders would be willing to invest in the Key Business Outcomes. For the ArtGalore digital art gallery, we considered an investment as follows:

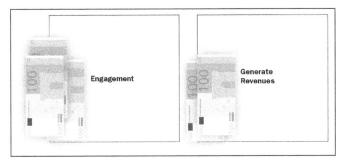

Business outcome	Engagement	Generated revenue
Invested amount	300	200

Based on our preceding user story map, we can create a sample list of feature ideas (given as follows). I am calling them ideas because these are not yet confirmed to be product features:

Feature ideas that meet business outcomes:

1. Premium art buyers can sign up to receive a newsletter with details of upcoming art shows, artists, and artworks

2. All art buyers can choose one or more artworks listed in the newsletter and purchase them

3. Smart recommendations for artworks to include in newsletter (internal)

4. Existing buyers can enter a lucky draw to meet an artist of the month

5. Auto-create newsletter content instead of having to prepare newsletter manually (internal)

Now, how do we prioritize these features based on value? Are features one and two equally important to build? What if we could determine the exact value for each feature? This can be determined using educated guesses! We can try to get all scientific about estimations, but that's exactly what they are—estimates. So why not estimate the value of a feature's impact on business outcomes?

Here's how to go about making a feature impact estimation: product managers, along with business stakeholders, estimate the impact of each feature on the Key Business Outcomes. They rate each feature on a scale of 0-10. The rating indicates the extent of the impact each feature can have on each invested business outcome. For instance, what impact will "existing buyers can enter a lucky draw to meet an artist of the month" have on engagement and generated revenue?

Stakeholders evaluate this based on how they envision the feature to be delivered. We could base our evaluation on data, insights from past user feedback, behavior, market trends, or even gut feeling! The key thing here is the conversations that happen at this stage. This is when stakeholders are actively discussing how to take a feature to market. They discuss the value that this feature can offer to the users. They are doing this without being constrained by the costs involved. So, let's say that stakeholders agree that we can predict that personalized, well-curated art catalogs would impact acquisitions at a 1 on the scale. Similarly, we can arrive at an estimated impact of this feature on engagement and generating revenue:

		Engagement	Generated revenue
Feature	**Invested amount**	300	200
Premium art buyers can sign up to receive a newsletter with details of upcoming art shows, artists, and artworks.	**Estimated impact**	7	3

This is an indicative rating. There are no right or wrong values for the estimated impact. We will be able to validate if our estimated ratings met the mark only when we generate outcomes by meeting defined success criteria. We will see more about success criteria in *Chapter 4*, *Plan for Success*.

So, the preceding table is showing what the digital art gallery business thinks the estimated impact for "premium art buyer can sign up to receive a newsletter with details of upcoming art shows, artists and artworks" will be. They expect this idea to create a lot of engagement (ranked 7 for estimated impact on the scale of 0 to 10), and they expect it to have a little impact on generating revenue (ranked 3 for estimated impact on the scale of 0 to 10). Similarly, we can assess every feature against the business outcomes. The following is a representative illustration of the estimated impact per feature idea against each business outcome:

		Engagement	Generated revenue
Feature idea	Invested amount	300	200
#1 – Premium art buyers can sign up to receive a newsletter with details of upcoming art shows, artists, and artworks.	Estimated impact	7	3
#2 – All art buyers can choose one or more artworks listed in the newsletter and purchase them.	Estimated impact	5	3
#3 – Smart recommendations for artworks to include in newsletter (internal).	Estimated impact	5	0
#4 – Existing buyers can enter a lucky draw to meet an artist of the month.	Estimated impact	6	0
#5 – Auto-create newsletter content instead of having to prepare newsletter manually (internal).	Estimated impact	0	0

We're still one step away from arriving at a comparative value. We can now calculate weighted scores based on the invested amount (weight) and estimated impact scores. For instance, for feature one, the total value score would be *(300x7) + (200x3) = 2700 points*. Similarly, we can calculate the value for every feature and arrive at a table as follows:

		Engagement	Generated revenue	Engagement weighted score	Generate revenue weighted score	Value score
Feature idea	Invested amount >>	**300**	**200**	(Invested amount X estimated impact)	(Invested amount X estimated impact)	**Sum of weighted score**
1. Premium art buyer can sign up to receive a newsletter with details of upcoming art shows, artists, artworks.	Estimated impact rating >>	7	3	2100	600	2700
2. All art buyers can choose one or more artworks listed in thr newsletter and purchase them	Estimated impact rating >>	5	3	1500	600	2100
3. Smart recommendations for artworks to include in newsletter (internal)	Estimated impact rating >>	5	0	1500	0	1500
4. Existing buyers can enter a lucky draw to meet an artist of the month	Estimated impact rating >>	6	0	1800	0	1800
5. Auto create newsletter content instead of having to prepare newsletter manually (internal)	Estimated impact rating >>	0	0	0	0	0

Now, when we sort the results based on the total impact scores for each feature, we can figure out the most valuable feature. The most impactful features are the ones with the highest impact scores.

Visualizing our priorities using a 2 × 2 matrix

A cost-value 2 × 2 matrix is another great tool for visualizing the relative priorities of features.

A 2 × 2 matrix captures the value on one axis and the cost on the other. Together they form two quadrants, which can be depicted as follows:

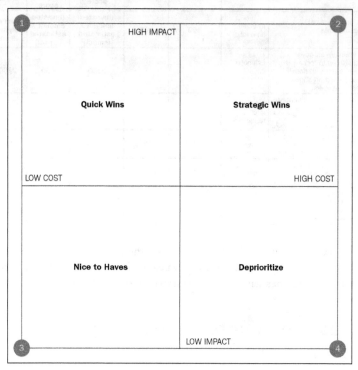

Typically, the costs are a combination of development effort and technical complexity, while impact is the impact that the feature idea could have on Key Business Outcomes and customer value. However, we now have features already prioritized for us, based on the projected business outcomes represented as a number value. Also, we know that the maximum impact that a feature can have is 5000 (500 × 10, where 500 is the maximum amount that can be invested and 10 is the maximum estimated impact rating), and the lowest is zero.

We can now arrange our feature cards based on their relative impact. We don't yet know the costs associated with building each feature. The following is a representation of our feature ideas listed earlier in the 2 × 2 matrix, purely based on their impact scores:

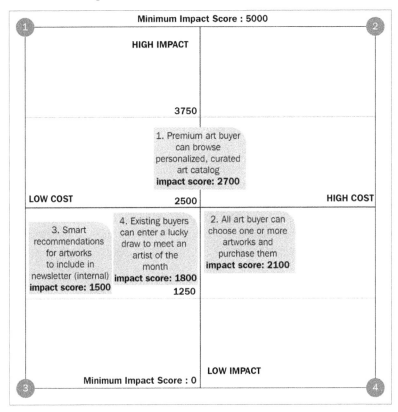

Feature idea 5 is not in the grid since it was estimated to have zero impact on Key Business Outcomes. So, feature 5 is already out of our backlog. Now we need to find the best way to implement these four feature ideas. To do this, we need to define what success means for each feature idea, and then evaluate the costs associated with them.

Summary

In this chapter, we learned that the product backlog must include only those feature ideas that will have a significant impact on Key Business Outcomes. If a feature idea is not expected to meet Key Business Outcomes, then there is no value in spending any effort in exploring the idea. Effort here is analysis, viability testing, market research, and so on. Needless to say, we need data and insights to make a better estimate about the impact of a feature idea, but sifting through this ensures that our product backlog stays lean. We can then steer all our efforts toward the most valuable outcomes, both for the customer and for the business. Impact scores are only one aspect of determining the effectiveness of a feature. There are costs associated with implementing a feature idea.

Before we venture into the costs of building a feature, we need to define success criteria. We must define what indicators will tell us not just if our estimated value impact is correct, but also where we failed to find success. What makes us happy? Is it user experience? Is it how quickly users can access our content? Is it the quality of our content? Is it the lack of complaints about mismatched content? Let's find out more about defining success criteria in the next chapter.

4

PLAN FOR SUCCESS

Until now, in the Impact Driven Product development cycle, we have arrived at a shared understanding of Key Business Outcomes and feature ideas that can help us to deliver value to our customers and maximize the impact on the KBOs. The next step is for us to identify what success means to us. For the kind of impact that we predict our feature idea to have on the KBOs, how do we ensure that every aspect of our business is aligned to enable that success? We may also need to make technical trade-offs to ensure that all effort on building the product is geared toward creating a satisfying end-to-end product experience.

When individual business functions take trade-off decisions in silo, we could end up creating a broken product experience or improvising the product experience where no improvement is required. For a business to be able to align on trade-offs that may need to be made on technology, it is important to communicate not just what is possible within business constraints but also what is not achievable. It is not necessary for the business to know or understand the specific best practices, coding practices, design patterns, and so on, that product engineering may apply. However, the business needs to know the value or the lack of value realization, of any investment that is made in terms of costs, effort, resources, and so on.

This chapter addresses the following topics:

- The need to have a shared view of what success means for a feature idea
- Defining the right kind of success criteria
- Creating a shared understanding of technical success criteria

> *"If you want to go quickly, go alone. If you want to go far,*
> *go together. We have to go far — quickly."*
>
> *Al Gore*

Planning for success doesn't come naturally to many of us. Come to think of it, our heroes are always the people who averted failure or pulled us out of a crisis. We perceive success as 'not failing,' but when we set clear goals, failures don't seem that important. We can learn a thing or two about planning for success by observing how babies learn to walk. The trigger for walking starts with babies getting attracted to, say, some object or person that catches their fancy. They decide to act on the trigger, focusing their full attention on the goal of reaching what caught their fancy. They stumble, fall, and hurt themselves, but they will keep going after the goal. Their goal is not about walking. Walking is a means to reaching the shiny object or the person calling to them. So, they don't really see walking without falling as a measure of success. Of course, the really smart babies know to wail their way to getting the said shiny thing without lifting a toe.

Somewhere along the way, software development seems to have forgotten about shiny objects, and instead focused on how to walk without falling. In a way, this has led to an obsession with following processes without applying them to the context and writing perfect code, while disdaining and undervaluing supporting business practices. Although technology is a great enabler, it is not the end in itself. When applied in the context of running a business or creating social impact, technology cannot afford to operate as an isolated function. This is not to say that technologists don't care about impact. Of course, we do.

Technologists show a real passion for solving customer problems. They want their code to change lives, create impact, and add value. However, many technologists underestimate the importance of supporting business functions in delivering value. I have come across many developers who don't appreciate the value of marketing, sales, or support. In many cases, like the developer who spent a year perfecting his code without acquiring a single customer (refer to *Chapter 2, Invest in Key Business Outcomes*), they believe that beautiful code that solves the right problem is enough to make a business succeed. Nothing can be further from the truth.

Most of this type of thinking is the result of treating technology as an isolated function. There is a significant gap that exists between nontechnical folks and software engineers. On the one hand, nontechnical folks don't understand the possibilities, costs, and limitations of software technology. On the other hand, technologists don't value the need for supporting functions and communicate very little about the possibilities and limitations of technology. This expectation mismatch often leads to unrealistic goals and a widening gap between technology teams and the supporting functions. The result of this widening gap is often cracks opening in the end-to-end product experience for the customer, thereby resulting in a loss of business. Bridging this gap of expectation mismatch requires that technical teams and business functions communicate in the same language, but first they must communicate.

What does success mean to us?

In order to set the right expectations for outcomes, we need the collective wisdom of the entire team. We need to define and agree upon what success means for each feature and to each business function. This will enable teams to set up the entire product experience for success. Setting **specific, measurable, achievable, realistic, and time-bound (SMART)** metrics can resolve this.

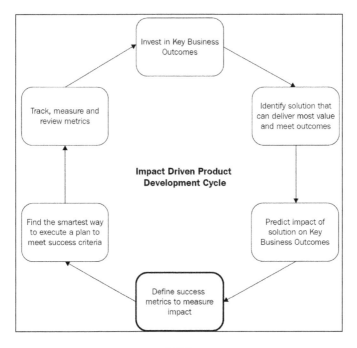

We cannot decouple our success criteria from the impact scores we arrived at earlier. So, let's refer back to the following table that we derived in *Chapter 3, Identify the Solution and its Impact on Key Business Outcomes*, for the ArtGalore digital art gallery:

Feature idea	Invested Amount >>	Engagement 300	Generated Revenue 200	Engagement Weighted Score (Invested Amount X Estimated Impact)	Generated Revenue Weighted Score (Invested Amount X Estimated Impact)	Impact Scores Sum of Weighted scores
1. Premium art buyer can sign up to receive the newsletter with details of upcoming art shows, artists, artworks.	Invested Impact Rating >>	7	3	2100	600	2700
2. All art buyers can choose one or more artworks listed in the newsletter and purchase them	Invested Impact Rating >>	5	3	1500	600	2100
3. Smart recommendations for artworks to include in newsletter (internal)	Invested Impact Rating >>	5	0	1500	0	1500
4. Existing buyers can enter a lucky draw to meet an artist of the month	Invested Impact Rating >>	6	0	1800	0	1800
5. Auto create newsletter content instead of having to prepare newsletter manually (internal)	Invested Impact Rating >>	0	0	0	0	0

The estimated impact rating was an indication of how much impact the business expected a feature idea to have on the Key Business Outcomes. If you recall, we rated this on a scale of 0 to 10. When the estimated impact of a Key Business Outcomes is less than five, then the success criteria for that feature is likely to be less ambitious. For example, the estimated impact of "existing buyers can enter a lucky draw to meet an artist of the month" toward generating revenue is zero. What this means is that we don't expect this feature idea to bring in any revenue for us or put in another way, revenue is not the measure of success for this feature idea. If any success criteria for generating revenue does come up for this feature idea, then there is a clear mismatch in terms of how we have prioritized the feature itself.

For any feature idea with an estimated impact of five or above, we need to get very specific about how to define and measure success. For instance, the feature idea "existing buyers can enter a lucky draw to meet an artist of the month" has an estimated impact rating of six towards engagement. This means that we expect an increase in engagement as a measure of success for this feature idea. Then, we need to define what "increase in engagement" means. My idea of "increase in engagement" can be very different from your idea of "increase in engagement." This is where being S.M.A.R.T. about our definition of success can be useful.

Success metrics are akin to user story acceptance criteria. Acceptance criteria define what conditions must be fulfilled by the software in order for us to sign off on the success of the user story. Acceptance criteria usually revolve around use cases and acceptable functional flows. Similarly, success criteria for feature ideas must define what indicators can tell us that the feature is delivering the expected impact on the KBO. Acceptance criteria also sometimes deal with NFRs (nonfunctional requirements). NFRs include performance, security, and reliability.

In many instances, nonfunctional requirements are treated as independent user stories. I also have seen many teams struggle with expressing the need for nonfunctional requirements from a customer's perspective. In the early days of writing user stories, the tendency for myself and most of my colleagues was to write NFRs from a system/application point of view. We would say, "this report must load in 20 seconds," or "in the event of a network failure, partial data must not be saved." These functional specifications didn't tell us how/why they were important for an end user. Writing user stories forces us to think about the user's perspective. For example, in my team we used to have interesting conversations about why a report needed to load within 20 seconds. This compelled us to think about how the user interacted with our software.

Some years ago, a friend of mine, who was working as part of a remote delivery team with little access to the real end users, narrated an interesting finding. Her team had been given a mandate to optimize report performance. One of her team members got an opportunity to travel to the location of some customers and observed how they used their software. The prime functionality of their software was to generate reports. The users would walk in at the beginning of the day, switch on their computers, launch the software, initiate a report, and step out for their morning coffee. The software took a good 15 minutes to generate a report! By the time the users had their coffee and had come back, the reports were ready. The customers had changed their habits to suit the software! The real question was how were we to react to this finding? Should we fix the reports to run faster? Should we leave them as is and focus on building other valuable functionality for the customers? Should this be a decision that technology must make in isolation?

It is not uncommon for visionary founders to throw out very ambitious goals for success. Having ambitious goals can have a positive impact in motivating teams to outperform. However, throwing lofty targets around, without having a plan for success, can be counter-productive. For instance, it's rather ambitious to say, "Our newsletter must be the first to publish artworks by all the popular artists in the country," or that "Our newsletter must become the benchmark for art curation." These are really inspiring words, but can mean nothing if we don't have a plan to get there.

I've heard many eager founders tell product engineers that their product should work like Facebook or Twitter or be as intuitive as Google. This expectation is there from the first version of the product! What do we do when the first release of a product is benchmarked against a product that took 10 years in the making and is a million iterations in? This is what I meant earlier when I mentioned expectation mismatch. It is important to get nontechnical stakeholders on board to meet the ambitious goals they prescribe to their teams. For instance, one of the things I do in ideation workshops is to not discount an ambitious (and impossible) goal such as the one stated earlier. I write it up as an outcome to achieve, and press for stakeholders to lay out their plans for how they intend to support making this happen. For example, at the level of responsiveness, performance, intuitiveness, and feature richness they expect from the product in its first release, we would need a sufficiently large user base and source of revenue to justify the costs/effort that go into building it. What is the business team's plan to source revenue in time for the first release? How do they plan to get the user base again in time for the first release?

Even when a product's technology is its main differentiator, other supporting business functions need to also come together in order to amplify the effectiveness of the technology. Successful products are a result of a lot of small things that come together to create impact.

The general rule of thumb for this part of product experience planning is that when we aim for an ambitious goal, we also sign up to making it happen. Defining success must be a collaborative exercise carried out by all stakeholders. This is the playing field for deciding where we can stretch our goals, and for everyone to agree on what we're signing up to, in order to set the product experience up for success.

Defining success metrics

For every feature idea we came up with in *Chapter 3*, *Identify the Solution and its Impact on Key Business Outcomes*, we can create feature cards that look like the following sample. This card indicates three aspects about what success means for this feature. We are asking these questions: what are we validating? When do we validate this? What Key Business Outcomes does it help us to validate?

Feature name: Primium art buyer can sign up to receive the newsletter with details of upcoming art shows, artists, artworks.		
What will tell us we have succeeded?	**When should we validate this (after launching functionality)?**	**Which Key Business Outcome will it validate?**
60% of those who sign up for a monthly art catalog will attend the upcoming art show	1 month	Engagement
80% of those who sign up for a monthly art catalog will enquire about at least 1 artwork	3 months	Engagement
15% of those who sign up for a monthly art catalog will purchase at least 1 artwork	3 months	Revenues
Engagement: 7 Generated Revenues: 3 Impact Score: 2700		

The criteria for success demonstrates what the business anticipates as being a tangible outcome from a feature. It also demonstrates which business functions will support, own, and drive the execution of the feature. That's it! We've nailed it, right? Wrong.

Success metrics must be SMART, but how specific is the specific? The preceding success metric indicates that 80% of those who sign up for the monthly art catalog will enquire about at least one artwork. Now, 80% could mean 80 people, 800 people, or 8000 people, depending on whether we get 100 sign-ups, 1000, or 10,000, respectively!

We have defined what external (customer/market) metrics to look for, but we have not defined whether we can realistically achieve this goal, given our resources and capabilities. The question we need to ask is: are we (as a business) equipped to handle 8000 enquiries? Do we have the expertise, resources, and people to manage this? If we don't plan in advance and assign ownership, our goals can lead to a gap in the product experience. When we clarify this explicitly, each business function could make assumptions.

When we say 80% of folks will enquire about one artwork, the sales team is thinking that around 50 people will enquire. This is what the sales team at ArtGalore is probably equipped to handle. However, marketing is aiming for 750 people and the developers are planning for 1000 people. So, even if we can attract 1000 enquiries, sales can handle only 50 enquiries a month! If this is what we're equipped for today, then building anything more could be wasteful. We need to think about how we can ramp up the sales team to handle more requests. The idea of drilling into success metrics is to gauge whether we're equipped to handle our success. So, maybe our success metric should be that we expect to get about 100 sign-ups in the first three months and between 40-70 folks enquiring about artworks after they sign up. Alternatively, we can find a smart way to enable sales to handle higher sales volumes.

In *Chapter 3*, *Identify the Solution and its Impact on Key Business Outcomes*, we created user story maps that addressed how internal business functions tie in to the feature idea. We don't take an outside-in view alone. We also need to define metrics for our inside-out view. This means that to chart a product experience strategy for this feature idea, we need more than just the software product specs. Before we write up success metrics, we should be asking a whole truckload of questions that determine the before-and-after of the feature.

We need to ask the following questions:

- What will the monthly catalog showcase?
- How many curated art items will be showcased each month?
- What is the nature of the content that we should showcase? Just good high-quality images and text, or is there something more?
- Who will put together the catalog?
- How long must this person/team(s) spend to create this catalog?
- Where will we source the art for curation?
- Is there a specific date each month when the newsletter needs to go out?
- Why do we think 80% of those who sign up will enquire? Is it because of the exclusive nature of art? Is it because of the quality of presentation? Is it because of the timing? What's so special about our catalog?
- Who handles the incoming enquiries? Is there a number to call or is it via email?
- How long would we take to respond to enquiries?
- If we get 10,000 sign-ups and receive 8000 enquiries, are we equipped to handle these? Are these numbers too high? Can we still meet our response time if we hit those numbers?

- Would we still be happy if we got only 50% of folks who sign up enquiring? What if it's 30%? When would we throw away the idea of the catalog?

This is where the meat of feature success starts taking shape. We need a plan to uncover underlying assumptions and set ourselves up for success. It's very easy for folks to put out ambitious metrics without understanding the before-and-after of the work involved in meeting that metric. The intent of a strategy should be to set teams up for success, not for failure.

Often, ambitious goals are set without considering whether they are realistic and achievable or not. This is so detrimental that teams eventually resort to manipulating the metrics or misrepresenting them, playing the blame game, or hiding information. Sometimes teams try to meet these metrics by deprioritizing other stuff. Eventually, team morale, productivity, and delivery take a hit. Ambitious goals, without the required capacity, capability, and resources to deliver, are useless.

The following is a sample success metric for the same feature, now revised to include internal operational metrics, and who owns each metric:

Feature name: Primium art buyer can sign up to receive the newsletter with details of upcoming art shows, artists, artworks.			
What will tell us we have succeeded?	**When should we validate this (after launching functionality)?**	**Who will own this?**	**Which outcomes will it validate?**
We will target 150 existing customers to sign up for newsletter.	1 week	Marketing, Customer Relationship, CEO	Engagement
60% of those who sign up for a monthly art catalog will attend the upcoming art show	1 months	Marketing team	Engagement
80% of those who sign up for a monthly art catalog will enquire about at least 1 artwork	3 months	Customer Relationship, Sales	Engagement
15% of those who sign up for a monthly art catalog will purchase at least 1 artwork	6 months	Sales/Customer Relationship	Revenues
Newsletter will have at least 20 curated artworks from 3 different categories.	Every month for 3 months	Marketing, Content, Art Curation	Engagement
Newsletter will be shipped out on 2nd of every month.	Every month for 3 months	Marketing, Tech and Content	Engagement
We will require less than 2 days to put together content.	Every month for 3 months	Content, Tech	?
All enquiries will be responded to within 1 day	Every month for 3 months	Sales/Customer Relationship	Revenues
Engagement: 7	Generated Revenues: 3		Impact Score: 2700

In the preceding sample, there is one success metric (grayed out) that we cannot link to desired business outcomes. So, this deprioritizes those metrics automatically. While these goals may be desirable to achieve, they are not something we have invested in for the current plan. For instance, the goal of putting together content in less than two days is an operational metric, which has not been invested as a Key Business Outcomes. So, we can discard that from our list of metrics to validate. We can further refine this to indicate success metrics as follows:

Feature name: Primium art buyer can sign up to receive the newsletter with details of upcoming art shows, artists, artworks.			
What will tell us we have succeeded?	**When should we validate this (after launching functionality)?**	**Who will own this?**	**Which outcomes will it validate?**
We will target 150 existing customers to sign up for newsletter.	1 week	Marketing, Customer Relationship, CEO	Engagement
60% of those who sign up for a monthly art catalog will attend the upcoming art show	1 months	Marketing team	Engagement
80% of those who sign up for a monthly art catalog will enquire about at least 1 artwork	3 months	Customer Relationship, Sales	Engagement
15% of those who sign up for a monthly art catalog will purchase at least 1 artwork	6 months	Sales/Customer Relationship	Revenues
Newsletter will have at least 20 curated artworks from 3 different categories.	Every month for 3 months	Marketing, Content, Art Curation	Engagement
Newsletter will be shipped out on 2nd of every month.	Every month for 3 months	Marketing, Tech and Content	Engagement
All enquiries will be responded to within 1 day	Every month for 3 months	Sales/Customer Relationship	Revenues
Engagement: 7	Generated Revenues: 3		Impact Score: 2700

Now, we have yet to decide whether this feature idea, shown in the preceding image fully or partially, will be part of a digital solution. This will be decided based on cost (time, effort, money, capabilities, and so on).

Mismatch in expectations from technology

Every business function needs to align toward the Key Business Outcomes and conform to the constraints under which the business operates. In our example here, the deadline is for the business to launch this feature idea before the Big Art show. So, meeting timelines is already a necessary measure of success.

The other indicators of product technology measures could be quality, usability, response times, latency, reliability, data privacy, security, and so on. These are traditionally clubbed under NFRs (nonfunctional requirements). They are indicators of how the system has been designed or how the system operates, and are not really about user behavior. There is no aspect of a product that is nonfunctional or without a bearing on business outcomes. In that sense, nonfunctional requirements are a misnomer. NFRs are really technical success criteria. They are also a business stakeholder's decision, based on what outcomes the business wants to pursue.

In many time and budget-bound software projects, technical success criteria trade-offs happen without understanding the business context or thinking about the end-to-end product experience.

Let's take a couple of examples: our app's performance may be okay when handling 100 users, but it could take a hit when we get to 10,000 users. By then, the business has moved on to other priorities and the product isn't ready to make the leap.

We can also think about cases where a product was always meant to be launched in many languages, but the Minimum Viable Product was designed to target users of one language only. We want to expand to other countries, and there will be significant effort involved in enabling the product, and operations to scale and adapt to this. Also, the effort required to scale software to one new location is not the same as the effort required to scale that software to 10 new locations. This is true of operations as well, but that effort is more relatable since it has more to do with people, process, and operations. So, the business is ready to accept the effort needed to set up scalable processes, and hire, train, and retain people. The problem is that the expectations of the technology are so misplaced that the business assumes that the technology can scale with minimal investment and effort. The limitations of technology can be sometimes perceived as lack of skills/capability of the technology team.

Plan for Success

This depends on how each team can communicate the impact of doing or not doing something today in terms of a cost tomorrow. What that means is that engineering may be able to create software that can scale to 5000 users with minimal effort, but in order to scale to 500,000 users, there's a different level of magnitude required. The frame of reference can be vastly skewed here. In the following figure, the increase in the number of users correlates to an increase in costs:

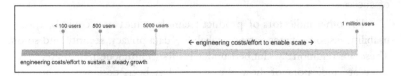

Let's consider a technology that is still in the realm of research, such as artificial intelligence, image recognition, or face recognition. With market-ready technology (where technology viability has been proven and can be applied to business use cases), in these domains, it may be possible to get to a 50% accuracy in image matching with some effort. Going from 50% to 80% would require an equal amount of effort as that which was needed to get to 50% accuracy. However, going from 80% to 90% accuracy would be way more complicated, and we would see a significant increase in costs and effort. Every 1% increase after 90% would be herculean, or just near impossible, given where the current technology is in that field. For instance, the number of variations in image quality that need to be considered could be a factor. The amount of blur, image compression quality, brightness, missing pixels in an image, and so on can impact the accuracy of results (`https://arxiv.org/pdf/1710.01494.pdf`). Face recognition from video footage brings in even more dimensions of complexity. The following figure is only for illustrative purposes and is not based on actual data:

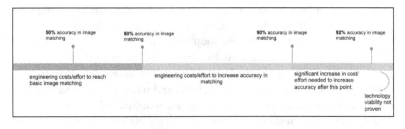

Now, getting our heads around something like this is going to be hard. We tend to create an analogy with a simple application. However, it's hard to get an apple-to-apple comparison of the effort involved in creating software. The potential of software is in the possibilities it can create, but that's also a bane because now that the bar is set so high, anything that lowers our expectations can be interpreted as: "Maybe you're not working hard enough at this!"

Sometimes the technology isn't even ready for this business case, or this is the wrong technology for this use case, or we shouldn't even be building this when there are products that can do this for us. Facial recognition technology with a 50% accuracy may suit a noncritical use case, but when applied to use cases for identifying criminals, or missing people, the accuracy needs are higher. In an online ads start-up that was built to show ads based on the images in the website content that a user was browsing, the context of the images was also important. The algorithm to show ads based on celebrity images worked with an accuracy that was acceptable to the business. The problem was that in some cases, the news item was related to a tragedy regarding a celebrity or an event where a celebrity was involved in a scandal. Showing the ads without the context could impact the image of the brand. This could be a potential threat for the online ads start-up looking to get new business. With a limited amount of resources and with a highly-skewed ratio of technology costs/viability, it remains a business decision on whether or not investment in technology is worth the value of the business outcomes. This is why I'm making the case that outcomes need to justify technology success criteria.

There is a different approach needed when building solutions for meeting short-term benefits, compared to how we might build systems for long-term benefits. It is not possible to generalize and make a case that just because we build an application quickly, that it is likely to be full of defects or that it won't be secure. By contrast, just because we build a lot of robustness into an application, this does not mean that it will make the product sell better. There is a cost to building something, and there is also a cost to not building something and a cost to a rework. The cost will be justified based on the benefits we can reap, but it is important for product technology and business stakeholders to align on the loss or gain in terms of the end-to-end product experience because of the technical approach we are taking today.

In order to arrive at these decisions, the business does not really need to understand design patterns, coding practices, or the nuanced technology details. They need to know the viability to meet business outcomes. This viability is based on technology possibilities, constraints, effort, skills needed, resources (hardware and software), time, and other prerequisites. What we can expect and what we *cannot* expect must both be agreed upon. In every scope-related discussion, I have seen that there are better insights and conversations when we highlight what the business/customer does *not* get from this product release. When we only highlight what value they will get, the discussions tend to go toward improvising on that value. When the business realizes what it doesn't get, the discussions lean toward improvising the end-to-end product experience.

Should a business care that we wrote unit tests? Does the business care what design patterns we used or what language or software we used? We can have general guidelines for healthy and effective ways to follow best practices within our lines of work, but best practices don't define us, outcomes do.

Cost of technical trade-offs

In the nonprofit where I was leading the product team, we launched a self-service kiosk to approve loans for people from rural India, after they clear an assessment on basic financial concepts, which was also offered through the kiosk. The solution involved so many facets of complexity. It had to be multilingual (there are 22 languages spoken in India, and an even greater number of dialects) and work in a low internet bandwidth (including literacy education videos and assessments). Many of the target users were illiterate or semiliterate and had not actively used touchscreens.

In addition, we had to ensure that we could remotely monitor, maintain, and support our kiosk software since we had no people or budgets to afford any travel. We also had to worry about security, our devices being tampered with, and that the devices had to be installed in buildings without climate control. We used Aadhar biometric authentication for our users and there were fingerprint scanners, thermal printers, and iris scanners, along with an Android tablet that served as the kiosk. On top of this, we employed machine learning to approve loans for people from rural India.

With so many moving parts, we had to prioritize our product launch. If we had to take a call on this from an isolated technology perspective, we would call out a minimal viable product with support for one language using manual approvals for loans, targeting Tier II cities with better internet and so on. However, the business context was that the nonprofit was trying to change the ecosystem of micro and peer-to-peer financing in a market that was being grossly neglected or abused by mainstream players (https://www.rangde.org/swabhimaan). The success of the solution was in how the rural folks adopted the self-service model, and how the nonprofit could get a foothold in areas where mainstream players weren't willing to venture. Our Impact Driven Product included all of these technical success criteria stated earlier.

We mercilessly cut down on functional flows, simplified our designs without remorse, and put in a lot of effort in understanding and learning about our target users. The product had the support for multiple languages, remote monitoring and maintenance, hardware that could secure our devices, software that worked in low internet bandwidth, a user interface that included audio prompts in multiple languages, and a machine learning algorithm that focused on reasons to approve a loan rather than to find reasons not to. We built all this in four months and launched it in three rural villages in different parts of India.

This would have not been possible if we had not looked at an end-to-end experience, including operations, recording audio messages, finding hardware and device partners and advisors, and ensuring every moving part moved toward the same Key Business Outcomes—adoption and sustainable operations.

Success metrics discussions are the best forums for adding value, not just by communicating what's possible but also by bringing out the opportunity cost of not building something. Product engineering needs to own the 'how' of the product. In some cases, this means taking a longer-term view on core technology foundations. There isn't a real choice between building fast and building right; sometimes, we need to do both simultaneously.

We should stop viewing engineering as an isolated function that does what it's told to do. Today, implementation decisions are either being forced down by a business that doesn't understand tech possibilities or those decisions are being made in isolation by technology without understanding business context. We should also stop getting fixated on coding practices and processes or lamenting about being unable to refactor code. If quick-and-dirty code can amply meet business outcomes, then there is no reason for us to fix it. Similarly, if the core of a technology-driven product needs a lot more attention, then technologists should find the best way to meet business outcomes with the least wasteful effort. At the same time, they should be able to own, steer, and set the direction for the business outcomes through the most valuable interventions.

Defining technical success criteria

So, in our art marketplace example, we can think of a couple of metrics that can be owned by product technology. For instance, ease of sign up or thinking of a mobile-first experience.

Feature name: Primium art buyer can sign up to receive the newsletter with details of upcoming art shows, artists, artworks.

What will tell us we have succeeded?	When should we validate this (after launching functionality)?	Who will own this?	Which outcomes will it validate?
We will target 150 existing customers to sign up for newsletter.	1 week	Marketing, Customer Relationship, CEO	Engagement
60% of those who sign up for a monthly art catalog will attend the upcoming art show	1 months	Marketing team	Engagement
80% of those who sign up for a monthly art catalog will enquire about at least 1 artwork	3 months	Customer Relationship, Sales	Engagement
15% of those who sign up for a monthly art catalog will purchase at least 1 artwork	6 months	Sales/Customer Relationship	Revenues
Newsletter will have at least 20 curated artworks from 3 different categories.	Every month for 3 months	Marketing, Content, Art Curation	Engagement
Newsletter will be shipped out on 2nd of every month.	Every month for 3 months	Marketing, Tech and Content	Engagement
All enquiries will be responded to within 1 day	Every month for 3 months	Sales/Customer Relationship	Revenues
Subscribers should be able to read the newsletter on their mobiles	At Launch	Product Tech	Engagement
Engagement: 7	Generated Revenues: 3		Impact Score: 2700

Summary

In this chapter, we learned that before commencing on the development of any feature idea, there must be a consensus on what outcomes we are seeking to achieve. The success metrics should be our guideline for finding the smartest way to implement a feature. The conversations at the stage of defining the success metrics should enable a shared understanding of what success means, how we see all the parts coming together to meet the same Key Business Outcomes, and our limitations and possibilities. This is true of not just technical success criteria, but for every business function.

In the next chapter, we will figure out the smartest way to meet success metrics.

5

IDENTIFY THE IMPACT DRIVEN PRODUCT

In the past few chapters, we saw how to evaluate the impact of feature ideas and define our success metrics. While defining success metrics, we were able to identify the different aspects of a business that need to come together to weave a delightful end-to-end product experience. This is the first step in creating a plan of execution for a feature idea, but there are many ways in which we can create the product and deliver value. Businesses strive to create products that provide lasting value for their customers. The Impact Driven Product for a business is not just about something that works. It is about what creates the most value. Product development should be open to consider, compare, and evaluate the value of building something from scratch versus buying an existing solution versus the necessity of building anything at all.

This chapter addresses the following topics:

- Value mapping
- Defining the Impact Driven Product
- Understanding the risks and costs of implementing a feature idea

Understanding product impact

"You mustn't be afraid to dream a little bigger, darling."

Eames, Inception

When I was in school, my uncle took us for a walk. He started talking about the house he was building. My dad had also just bought a house, and I was quite excited about the prospect of living in our own place. We were one of the first few people in the family who had ventured to buy a property. My uncle paused and asked me why he and my dad were able to buy a house, while our grandparents couldn't. I didn't blink before answering, "You both make more money." My uncle laughed so hard, and said, "No, we don't. We just have better access to loans." Sure enough, home loans opened up a lifetime goal for many.

Until a couple of decades ago, taking photos for pleasure was accessible only to those who could afford a camera. The alternative was to visit a photo studio. Every family had a similar looking family picture. I even read somewhere the story of parents who had taken a photo of only their firstborn. Every other child was shown the same photo as their childhood photo! Of course, mobile phones changed all that. A century ago, knowledge was restricted to a privileged few. Schools, libraries, and now the internet have democratized education.

Disruption happens when products impact people's lives in ways that were hitherto unrealized. Often, even creators cannot foresee these impacts. Visionaries can imagine a world in a way that is not bound by today's scarcity, and the disruption is a by-product of ambitious goals. Today's technological advances, infrastructure capabilities, talent, and opportunities make it possible for more of us to dream bigger. Success or failure depends on adoption and execution.

What minimum viability attempted to inculcate was a practice of building just what was enough to satisfy early adopters. The intent was to validate the riskiest hypotheses, without running out of runway. The riskiest hypotheses could be about technology viability, market adoption, revenue generation, and the overall business model itself.

We translated minimum viability to suggest that "we have limited resources. We don't know what will work. Let's build a product that is small enough to tell us if our idea works, without burning our resources." This is not at all a bad idea and is in fact the right way to approach untested waters. However, when employing market-ready technology (where technology viability has been proven and can be applied to business use cases), this mindset about building as little as possible can be limiting. We cannot build an ambitious business with a minimum product experience. Our mindset should shift to "we have ambitious goals. We don't know what will work. Let's deliver as much value to our customers, while generating as much value for the business. We find a way to make this work or we die trying!"

We need to change our mindset and leap for success, instead of bracing against failures. This does not mean that we have to build the whole gamut of functionality. It only means that we must be smart about building the most impactful functionality, without compromising on creating a delightful product experience.

Product teams must continue to explore the best way to deliver impact. This does not mean that we need to build everything from scratch. Our value is in being able to see the big picture and set up the business, customers, and the product for success. For this, we need to write the sheet music, not be the solo pianist. Defining business outcomes and the success metrics at a high level gives us a good handle on the value of a product experience. It also gives us an idea of the riskiest hypotheses we need to validate. Now we need to establish the cost of creating that product experience.

The cost of creating an impactful product experience

While business sponsors bet on business outcomes, they expect a good return on their investment (ROI). This investment was to build the most impactful product experience. Cost is a factor when evaluating the ROI, but it does not have to be a deciding factor.

Our capacity to deliver, drives the trade-offs we make. We need to the set the bar on product experience outcomes high enough, but at the same time, set ourselves up for success. Now we have to figure out how to succeed without burning all our resources (or running out of money). There is cost involved in building (people, skills, resources, support, and so on). There is also risk and we will incur risk by *not* building something today. It is important to have insights on missed opportunity, the cost of a rework, the cost of a repair, and so on. Once we identify our risks, we can choose to invest more to mitigate them or choose to live with the risks:

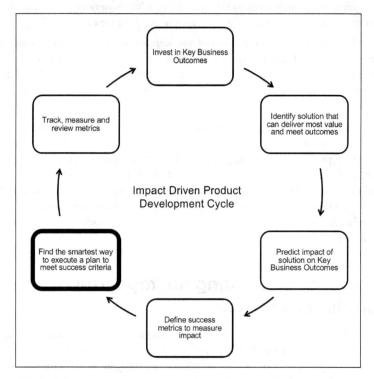

To find the smartest way to create a product experience, product teams need to consider the following:

- Value mapping
- Our Impact Driven Product
- Deciding to build, buy, or not at all
- The cost of a digital solution
- The risks of *not* building

Defining the Impact Driven Product

At this point, we have an idea about the functionality we need for meeting ArtGalore's Key Business Outcomes. We already have the high-level user story map defined:

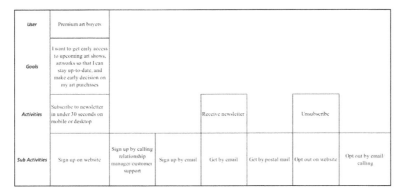

We also have prioritized the features that we need to build in order to meet the business outcomes:

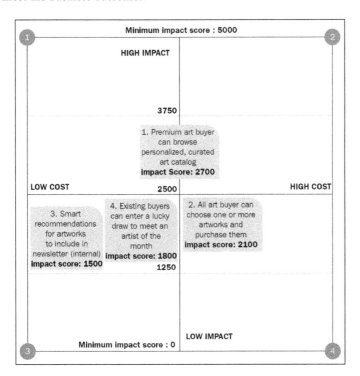

We have success criteria for each feature:

Feature name: Primium art buyer can sign up to receive the newsletter with details of upcoming art shows, artists, artworks.

What will tell us we have succeeded?	When should we validate this (after launching functionality)?	Who will own this?	Which outcomes will it validate?
We will target 150 existing customers to sign up for newsletter.	1 week	Marketing, Customer Relationship, CEO	Engagement
60% of those who sign up for a monthly art catalog will attend the upcoming art show	1 months	Marketing team	Engagement
80% of those who sign up for a monthly art catalog will enquire about at least 1 artwork	3 months	Customer Relationship, Sales	Engagement
15% of those who sign up for a monthly art catalog will purchase at least 1 artwork	6 months	Sales/Customer Relationship	Revenues
Newsletter will have at least 20 curated artworks from 3 different categories.	Every month for 3 months	Marketing, Content, Art Curation	Engagement
Newsletter will be shipped out on 2ⁿᵈ of every month.	Every month for 3 months	Marketing, Tech and Content	Engagement
All enquiries will be responded to within 1 day	Every month for 3 months	Sales/Customer Relationship	Revenues
Subscribers should be able to read the newsletter on their mobile	At Lunch	Product Tech	Engagement
Engagement: 7	Generated Revenues: 3		Impact Score: 2700

The next step is to detail the user journeys for each feature. For this, we need to keep in mind the success criteria we're aiming for. These success criteria need to get woven into the product experience. We also need a way to measure and validate the success metrics.

Let's take a look at the feature that marketplace visitors can sign up to receive a monthly art catalog:

User	Premium art buyers							
Goals	I want to get early access to upcoming art shows, artworks so that I can stay up-to-date, and make early decision on my art purchases							
Activities	Subscribe to newsletter in under 30 seconds on mobile or desktop				Receive newsletter		Unsubscribe	
Sub Activities	Sign up on website	Sign up by calling relationship manager/ customer support		Sign up by email	Get by email	Get by postal mail	Opt out on website	Opt out by email/calling
	Launch on laptop	Launch website on mobile			Send email to email id stated on website		Get newsletter on email Inbox.	
	See option to get newsletter	See option to get newsletter			Receive auto confirmation response		Open email on laptop mobile, and view all content	
	Provide email	Provide email					Download newsletter attachment	
	Type in captcha, and prove not a robot	Type in captcha, and prove not a robot						
	Sign up	Sign up						
	See confirmation	See confirmation						
	Get activation email	Get activation email						
	Confirm	Confirm						
	Get Welcome email	Get Welcome email						

The activity "subscribers should be able to read newsletters through mobile or desktop" has captured the success metrics, but signing up is not enough. Receiving the actual newsletter, and then having an option to unsubscribe, are necessary to completing the end-to-end functionality.

We do know now that the success metric is defined by the ease of signing up. At this point, we would do well to explore if we should ask the user to sign up on the website and receive the newsletter through postal mail even! We could also explore if the option to unsubscribe is legally mandated. The important aspect here is to define the user journey. For instance, if a feature is not mandated by legal compliance, then that is a negotiable card for us now. It also depends on the target segment. So, we could still choose to not build a feature now and decide to manage the risk. The risk is not just because of legal noncompliance but also about how the brand can be perceived. There is a cost of risk associated with this, which will be captured in subsequent steps.

This negotiation is possible only where our success has no direct correlation with the functionality. At this stage, we want to elaborate all possible journeys for a user to meet their goal. There are many journeys to offering this product experience. For instance, any of the following is possible:

- Users can sign up on the website (desktop and mobile) and receive the newsletter by postal mail, with no option to unsubscribe
- Users can sign up on the website (desktop and mobile) and receive the newsletter by email, with no option to unsubscribe
- Users can sign up on website (desktop and mobile), receive the newsletter by postal mail, and unsubscribe online
- Users can sign up on the website (desktop and mobile), receive the newsletter by postal mail, and unsubscribe offline (call/email)

- Users can sign up on the website (desktop and mobile), receive the newsletter by email, and unsubscribe online
- Users can sign up on the website (desktop and mobile), receive the newsletter by email, and unsubscribe offline (call/email)
- Users can sign up by email and receive the newsletter by postal mail, with no option to unsubscribe
- Users can sign up by email and receive the newsletter by email, with no option to unsubscribe
- Users can sign up by email, receive the newsletter by postal mail, and unsubscribe online
- Users can sign up by email, receive the newsletter by postal mail, and unsubscribe offline (call/email)
- Users can sign up by email, receive the newsletter by email, and unsubscribe online
- Users can sign up by email, receive the newsletter by email, and unsubscribe offline (call/email)
- Users can sign up by calling and receive the newsletter by postal mail, with no option to unsubscribe
- Users can sign up by calling and receive the newsletter by email, with no option to unsubscribe
- Users can sign up by calling, receive the newsletter by postal mail, and unsubscribe online
- Users can sign up by calling, receive the newsletter by postal mail, and unsubscribe offline (call/email)
- Users can sign up by calling, receive the newsletter by email, and unsubscribe online
- Users can sign up by calling, receive the newsletter by email, and unsubscribe offline (call/email)

So, our Impact Driven Product for this feature is the one that offers the best possible user experience including the functionality that meets the success criteria, plus metrics to measure the success criteria. Before we decide the costs of building this, we need to map the value.

Value mapping

When creating a product experience, technology can play two roles. Firstly, technology can be a business enabler, where business operations or some parts of the core business, are complemented by digital solutions. Secondly, technology can be a differentiator. Here, software technology/digital solutions drive the core business.

It is important to internalize the difference between the two roles that technology plays in our business. Business enablers can bring a great deal of value to the business, but they play only a supporting role. Businesses can still exist without a digital enabler, although they may not thrive or scale, whereas, a differentiator is the core product itself. If the digital product doesn't exist, then there is no business to run. This is where the IP (intellectual property, which is the intangible value created from patents, copyright, or creativity) of a product is created.

So, business outcomes can be driven by digital solutions that are either enablers or differentiators. It is crucial to know if the feature that we are evaluating is a differentiator or an enabler. In the case of our newsletter, the content of the newsletter (our curated artworks and so on) forms our differentiators. However, the process to receive the newsletters isn't our differentiator. So, we can choose to build the simplest digital solution or leverage what already exists. At this point, let's say that to evaluate these four journeys is our best bet for creating an Impact Driven Product experience:

- Users can sign up by email, receive the newsletter by email, and unsubscribe online
- Users can sign up on the website (desktop and mobile), receive the newsletter by email, and unsubscribe online
- Users can sign up by email, receive the newsletter by postal mail, and unsubscribe online
- Users can sign up on the website (desktop and mobile), receive the newsletter by postal mail, and unsubscribe online

Deciding to build, buy, or not at all

We don't need to start coding every feature into the digital solution. During the early stages of product development, we must assess where to spend our capacity and resources. Often, both business sponsors and engineers get carried away by the possibilities that a digital solution can offer. Since we have now methodically established the business outcomes, the most important product features, and the success metrics to achieve, we need to find the right fitment of solutions.

Once we have established a differentiator or an enabler, we need to explore the possible options available to us. The first step is to decide if there is even any value in building the feature. We could also look for solutions outside (off-the-shelf products) or use an open source tool or outsource (to a noncore product development team). If our feature is an enabler and if our success metrics can be achieved by an off-the-shelf tool, then we should just proceed with finding the optimal tool.

In our example from the preceding story map, our feature is to ship out a newsletter. We need to assess how the content of the newsletter will be created. The value of the newsletter is in the content it offers to the art buyer. This is the differentiator, and hence we might do well to invest heavily in content building, rather than in the process. In this context, if we assess sending newsletters by postal mail versus sending them by email, then email seems to be the lightweight option.

Now, we can also explore the best way to allow users to sign up. Sending an email seems simple enough for users, but for them to discover our email address, they're likely to be already on the website. Also, it takes additional effort for someone to sort through the email requests and maintain this list. In this context, building a simple sign-in section on the existing website and mailing to the subscribed list, might be efficient. So, we might arrive at the following journey as the most valuable experience:

- Users can sign up on the website (desktop and mobile), receive the newsletter by email, and unsubscribe online

We need to have a way to track the success metrics. So, this also forms our digital solution. This tracking will be not just for the metrics related to signing up, but also for us to track how many of the users who signed up converted to enquiries or sales. Again, this is an assessment about an enabler/differentiator. While the data itself is privy to us, the process of capturing the metrics may not be our differentiator. So, there is an opportunity for us to explore off-the-shelf tools that can help us to capture and report metrics.

The cost of a digital solution

We get to this step only if we have established whether a feature is a differentiator or an enabler, but with no options or suboptimal options, for ready-made solutions. We need to assess if we can build this functionality in the time frame that we have (refer to *Chapter 6*, *Managing the Scope of an Impact Driven Product*).

This will help us to arrive at the costs that include (but are not limited to) the following:

- The development cost (time and people)
- Resources (software, assets, and hardware)
- Hosting
- Support and maintenance
- Training

Now we can drill down to the specifics of cost numbers. A quick-and-dirty solution might require higher maintenance. Compromise on user experience might require higher training investment. In some cases, pricing for hosting, an off-the-shelf solution needs to be worked out. However, our cost assessments can also be relative. So, we can box our feature costs into small, medium, or large buckets, or even rank them on a scale of 1-10 in terms of complexity (determined based on the preceding aspects).

Risks of not building something

In some cases, we may end up not meeting some functionality, because the cost of building is too high. Yet not building something might have a negative effect on the product experience. For instance, providing an unsubscribe option in a user's profile might involve higher development effort. This might increase the rank of this card from three to five (on a scale of ten). So, we decide that this is not the most critical functionality to build at the moment. The success criteria are not dependent on the ability to unsubscribe, but compliance requires us to offer the option. So, we are incurring a risk by not providing this option. We have to agree to invest in the cost of building this option the perfect way, or decide to incur the risk, or find a simpler way to do this. We further refine our journey as the most valuable experience, as shown here:

- Users can sign up on the website (desktop and mobile), receive the newsletter by email, and unsubscribe offline (email/call)

Risks are the items that can meet *all* success criteria needed today, but may incur a future cost. This could be due to any of the following reasons:

- Extensibility (can we build on this later?)
- User experience consistency
- User experience completeness
- Branding consistency
- Rework due to future scale/functional/compliance needs

This is not to be confused with a scope negotiation. This risk is an indication of the compromises we are making today, in the context of current internal and external constraints, in order to meet the Key Business Outcomes and success metrics. It would help to capture these risks as trackable cards in our risk backlog. We can revisit these risks later.

The items on the risk potential list should be reviewed, based on the impact they could have on the business outcomes. We can then choose to factor them into our cost of building or continue to keep them as open risks.

What if our costs are too high if we have to meet all success metrics? Should we attempt to deprioritize any success metric? This is a business decision to make. If the ratio of cost to impact isn't acceptable to the business, then we need to explore what is increasing our costs. Is it a technical approach we have taken, or are the goals so ambitious that we cannot achieve them? This means that the business needs to see so much value in the feature, in order to justify our costs. This then feeds back to the defining success metrics phase. We need to always set up and plan for success. It's all or nothing.

Estimates form a small part of this activity. Effort involved in building this feature will also add to the cost, but there is no reason for us to get precise numbers of the exact number of hours we would spend on building this, and compare them with past feature building and so on. This aspect about estimates and staying lean about our development processes is discussed in the third part of this book.

The cost-impact matrix

The cost-impact matrix can help us visualize the trade-offs and advantages we get by investing in a product feature. This can help us prioritize and prune our product backlog.

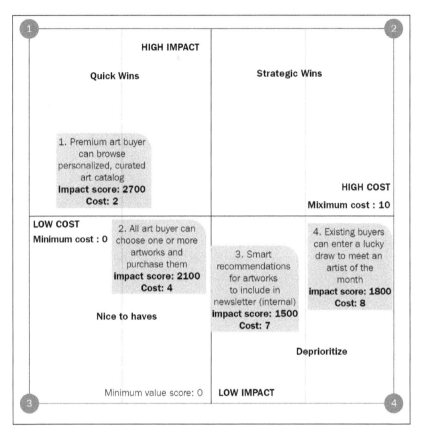

Based on the cost and previously determined business value scores, we now have a clear view of our prioritization matrix. The features in quadrant one are the quick wins (low cost / high value). Anything in quadrant four should not be picked up. Risk backlog, which exists outside of the quadrant, should include functionality or tasks that haven't been picked up now, but are likely to have an impact later. Also, this gives a clear view to the business sponsors of the costs they will incur when we need to build this functionality in the future.

Summary

All the analysis involved in defining the Impact Driven Product experience and ensuring that all business functions are aligned toward meeting the same Key Business Outcomes, as well as a view of costs, comes together in the Cost Impact matrix. The Cost Impact matrix offers a visually compelling view of how a feature's value compares to the cost of building it. This can enable decision-making around which feature ideas to pursue for immediate benefits and which ones to invest in, for longer-term strategic benefit. It also helps in analyzing trade-offs and functional scope, and therefore in determining whether a feature idea can be trimmed down or whether it's worth investing in a feature idea even though the costs are higher. Once the cost-impact comparison is done, the feature ideas can make it to the product backlog.

Now, we have our backlog ready, so let's go and build our product in the next chapter!

PART TWO

ARE WE BUILDING THE RIGHT PRODUCT?

6

MANAGING THE SCOPE OF AN IMPACT DRIVEN PRODUCT

In the previous chapter, we saw how to create a cost-impact matrix and determine the smartest way to deliver an Impact Driven Product. Now, these were a prioritized list of feature ideas, but when we have more feature ideas than we can possibly deliver within given business constraints, also accounting for external pressures, how do we decide which feature to launch? Also, within each feature, how do we determine the level of product completeness?

Business and market maturity determine the extent of product completeness we aim for. Unexplored markets, fuzzy business ideas, and untested technology need one approach to product building. Known business models and processes in established markets may require another approach. Exploring product/market fit with viable technology and untested business goals requires a different approach again.

In this regard, this chapter looks at the following topics:

- The need to understand the maturity of the business and the market landscape in order to determine the first version of the product to launch
- The inputs to consider for every subsequent release of the product
- Defining the scope for the product release

Are we there yet?

"Done is better than perfect."
Anonymous

I have been painting, sketching, and teaching art for many years now. As an artist, I find many similarities in excitement and challenges between planning a painting and managing a product. When an inspiration for a new painting descends, it is so energizing. I want to jump right in, splash paint on a canvas, and let the brush strokes take over. Sometimes, it feels almost like desperation. It's almost like this: if I don't capture the inspiration in my head and put it on a canvas swiftly, the inspiration will fizzle out.

Of course, making good art requires planning. There is a method to it. Paints don't dry at the pace you want them to. Proportions and perspectives don't fix themselves. Brushes and palettes don't take care of themselves. I have to slow down and plan the details. I need to work on the painting layer by layer, but this slowing down and deeply connecting with each layer of a painting has its downside. It creates a sort of obsession with details. There is a drive to stop at nothing but perfection. I have a tendency to keep improving on the painting, and never really feel satisfied. This dissatisfaction can be so blinding that sometimes I want to tear it all apart and start afresh.

Over time, I have come to learn the trick to avoiding this trap. The trick is to step back and evaluate. Sometimes, this evaluation requires feedback from others. I must throw away the brush when I find myself coming back and fixing a little speck of paint here and there. Forcing myself to stop prevents me from getting sucked into the abyss of seeking perfection. It helps me to look at the *big picture* (literally) and value it for what it is.

At the end of my painting process, I still put out something that I'm *reasonably* satisfied with. I can still identify a thousand mistakes in my painting: patched up corrections, less-than-perfect work, poor choice of colors, and all the other shortcomings. For someone looking at a completed artwork, the nuances of how it was made and the perfection of the painting techniques may be hidden. Also, art is very personal. So, the emotional appeal may matter more than the technique. Sometimes I might be very happy with how my painting turned out, but the people who I show it to may be unimpressed. Sometimes I might be underwhelmed about my painting, but those who see it may be excited. In my head, the gap between what I envisioned and what I could capture on canvas is big enough to create a sense of dissatisfaction forever.

Product building is a similar experience for many of us. How do we know when to stop obsessing about our product? How do we know if it's ready? What if we had a Goldilocks in each of us who told us, "This is just right!" The point is that we hardly ever feel this certain about when to launch and what to obsess about, if at all. There is no real way to know when we're *done*.

In fact, this uncertainty is magnified in product teams because it is usually one person's vision that the whole team is trying to translate into a product. It can be frustrating for both the team and for the visionary to work with each other. We're either over-engineering parts that we don't need to, or not fine-tuning the stuff that ought to be, or not going fast enough, and so on. The external market pressures don't make it any easier. The trick that works for me when I'm painting can help here too. It's important for product teams to step back and objectively assess if they are on the right track or not. We need to obsess about some details and at the same time, be willing to let some rough edges pass through. It is important to get the product out the door. Remember, *done is better than perfect.*

When we determine the scope of the product at the first launch, software teams consider two key concepts: fail fast and the idea of a Minimum Viable Product. These are both great ways to help the business to focus on what it seeks to validate. However, do these concepts apply to all stages of the business? Also, what are our pitfalls when these concepts are misapplied? Let's explore.

Faster is not always smarter

Getting it done is one thing, but getting it done on time is another thing altogether. The line between releasing something too soon or too late is quite blurry. There are many factors that determine when the product is ready to be released. This does not just apply at the first launch. This decision must be made when we launch every product milestone. Let's hold onto this thought for a moment and look at how the software development paradigm has shifted from a waterfall mindset to Agile.

We already saw in earlier chapters that one of the failures of the waterfall model is that the product gets stuck in development for too long. By the time we launch the product, any chance of responding to valuable feedback is lost or becomes too costly. The business scenarios have changed, the feedback loop is longer, and it's extremely difficult to respond quickly to feedback. With Agile, the idea of shorter releases is one of the crucial drivers. How soon can we release something to get feedback? The intent of shorter releases (and shorter Build-Measure-Learn loops) is to *fail fast*. While the sentiment is commendable, the implementation has some gaps.

Failing fast was meant as a way to test our riskiest propositions first and learn from them. It was not meant to hasten up our effort without thinking through the outcomes we expect from our effort. It was not about mindless speed, with an intent to fail. The problem, as with any other idea, is in how we choose to interpret and apply it.

We have translated *fail fast* as, "Let's put *something* out there real fast. If we fail, then we start over." Ideally, a short Build-Measure-Learn loop enables software teams to conserve their resources, and not waste much effort building stuff in advance. However, that works only when we know what we're validating. We need to define our riskiest propositions and our expected outcomes. When we don't define our outcomes first, we may be unable to learn anything of importance from our product. Product development cannot become about speed alone, without an understanding of outcomes. *Fail fast* should not trump *learn fast*.

This also impacts our process of working, such that we want feedback along every minor step of the way, without knowing it's value; for instance, showcasing every user story that is completed. I have been part of many Agile software development projects where stakeholder showcases were conducted religiously. A typical first iteration showcase of an Agile software services project might involve showcasing the 'Login story.' The stakeholders are often quite fired up about the first showcase. In my experience, we get a lot of feedback on the placement of the submit button in the login screen. We spend quite some time in discussion over whether to name it "Submit" or "Sign in" or "Login." Been there, done that!

We all feel super good about having done our bit in building iteratively, receiving feedback, and having involved business folks every step of the way, but is it of any use to anyone? Logging in to an application is a task. It is a pre-requisite to accomplishing anything of value inside the application. Logging in by itself adds no material user value. We have all probably written an "as a user, I want to log in, so that I can access the application" story at some point!

OK, I'm being a little unkind here. The intent of these teams has always been noble. Software teams are actively striving to get feedback at every step of the way, but the implementation of this is flawed. We need to go after valuable feedback, and not just any feedback. We cannot hope to get valuable feedback when we don't showcase anything of value. There is really nothing of value to learn from a login story. The login functionality by itself cannot be launched as a product. In fact, if anything, we probably wasted about an hour's time, in an iteration showcase meeting, discussing the merits of renaming the "Submit" button to "Login."

Minimum Viable Product (mvp)

The second concept that software teams take pride in is the **Minimum Viable Product** (**mvp**), which seeks to answer the question: what is the cheapest and fastest product that we can build to help us to learn something of value? My observation of software teams is that we use mvp as a scope management paradigm. When we have to do many things in the backlog and time/budgets are limited, we identify the mvp. Once again, the intent of releasing a usable product under given constraints is commendable, but an mvp defined based on the two dimensions of time and budget isn't really an mvp.

In early 2016, coach and consultant Henrik Kniberg came up with this drawing (https://blog.crisp.se/2016/01/25/henrikkniberg/making-sense-of-mvp). It has caught on quite well and is popular among Agile practitioners. As Henrik writes in his blog, "The picture is a metaphor. It is not about actual car development, it is about product development in general, using a car as a metaphor."

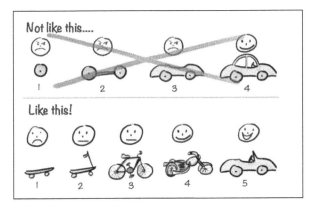

The preceding diagram shows Agile and lean development and the idea of the mvp. It is a good representation of a shifting mindset in software teams. The "not like this" section essentially highlights the futility of the approach, where we release a login story. The equivalent here is that we released a wheel. It brings out the flaw in the iterative software development mindset. In Henrik's own words (from his blog), ".... the first row represents 'bastardized Agile.' Technically, it might be incremental and iterative delivery, but the absence of an actual feedback loop makes it very risky—and definitely not agile." He then goes on to explain how this should actually be done and what real mvp thinking should be. This is the second half of the picture titled "like this!"

Each iteration in this picture is delivering a product. Henrik prefers to call it the "Earliest Testable Product." When the goal is to travel from point A to point B, then the first iteration is the skateboard version. It's quick to build. It meets the goal. It can be built fast. It can be built cheap(er). It is usable.

The skateboard fits the mvp paradigm well:

- It is minimal, requires minimal resources, and it doesn't have frills. It has only what is needed to meet the goal
- It is viable. The underlying technology of travel is viable. (This means that with two pairs of wheels, each connected by an axle that can turn the wheels. The product can carry a passenger from point A to point B, without harming the passenger.)
- It is a product. It is usable. Someone will pay for this product.

It sounds perfect. Well, almost. The skateboard answers only the "what is the cheapest and fastest product that we can build?" part of the mvp question. The second part about learning something of value is sort of lost.

Missing pieces in the mvp model

Henrik's picture and its description of the mvp model is not really a practical representation of how a product can be launched in the market. I'm choosing this picture only because it succinctly captures the current mvp thinking. My critique is not of the picture, but of the mvp thinking itself in general. My first objection is with the problem statement. Business goals are not defined as "let's find the fastest way to travel from point A to point B." This statement is in the realm of research. Businesses have something more tangible. The goal statements are born out of something like: "I want to manufacture the most luxurious cars that will make people desire car travel, and have families look forward to long drives and road trips." For instance, the Tata Nano was meant to be an affordable family car that could be within the reach of Indian families who were then travelling on bikes. So, why would we build a skateboard to meet such a goal?

The questions that the mvp seeks to answer are as follows:

1. Is there a problem worth solving? Will anyone pay for a solution to the problem?

2. Is our technology viable? Does it solve the problem well for the target customer segment?

3. Is our business idea viable? Does it garner sufficient interest from the target customer segment?

4. Will our riskiest proposition nullify our biggest hypotheses? Will the failure of technology/business viability kill our business?

The mvp should help us decide between persisting or pivoting to a different target segment or a new business model. However, we still need to start with solving problems for a narrow target segment. mvp is not a proof of concept, nor is it a full-fledged product. It was meant to be the smallest thing we can put together to answer the preceding questions. In some cases, the mvp is not even a product. If technology viability is already proven, then let's not waste time building anything. We should rather spend all our effort validating the business idea and the riskiest proposition for the business model.

Can a skateboard help us to learn anything of value when we want to build a car? Will a consumer who wants to enjoy a luxury trip with their family adopt and give us valuable feedback about a skateboard? If you were a car manufacturer, would you launch a skateboard to your consumers? You might argue that Tatas wouldn't build a skateboard because there already are cars in the market. Well, exactly, but did the first car makers build a skateboard? What did car makers Benz and Daimler build? Was there a skateboard in the product development for the first cars? Not really.

A brief time lapse on car making

In the late 19th century, the innovation around internal combustion engines and fuel injection technologies began. The technology proved the existence of a viable solution that could be applied to a number of fields. Transport was one of them. The inventors/innovators were tinkering with the engines, trying to find the most compact, lightweight, and efficient system. The viability of engine technology opened up possibilities of replacing horse-driven carriages with human-controlled automobiles. The earliest version of a finished, usable automobile was an engine fitted onto a two-wheeled (cycle-like) frame. This was called the riding car (see the following image):

Source: http://media.daimler.com/marsMediaSite/en/instance/ko/
Mercedes-Benz-Classic-November-1885-Daimler-riding-car-travels-
from-Cannstatt-to-Untertuerkheim.xhtml?oid=9914922

An article about the car says, "The most important prerequisite for the riding car, simultaneously the world's first motorcycle, was Gottlieb Daimler's four-stroke, single-cylinder engine, which he registered for patent on 3 April, 1885. In the sum of its features, the riding car was the most important precursor to individual mobility, thereafter rendered possible by the advent of the automobile. It was proof on wheels that the internal combustion engine was capable of powering a road-going vehicle—and that a human being could fully control it."

The riding car was proof that a vehicle powered by an engine and controlled by a human was possible. The riding car had validated technology viability. It had cleared step one in the problem/solution fit stage from a technology perspective. Still, it hadn't yet shown the viability for the car makers who were competing with horse-driven carriages. This engine was still not viable for a four-wheel automobile. The target segment was quite different and the market needs of the target customers that car makers would go after was quite different. As Henrik Kniberg described, the riding car (two-wheeler) was the mvp for "human controllable automobiles." It proved that a solution for a problem worth solving existed. It also proved the technology viability.

However, there were quite a few other aspects to uncover for the car makers. Daimler and Benz's individual efforts in creating a three-wheel and four-wheel automobile respectively emphatically proved that the technology viability established by the riding car's engine could be applied to a different product with some modifications. There was a second wave of inventions and patents between the first riding car (two-wheeler) and the four-wheeled automobile (https://www.daimler.com/company/tradition/company-history/1886-1920.html).

The technology innovations in the engines proved that a human-controlled automobile was possible. Once the initial technology (of the engine) was proven to be viable, a host of vehicles started to sprout including motor boats, omnibuses, and cars. The power, acceleration, fuel material, and so on had a second wave of innovations that paved the way for a three-wheel and four-wheel version of the automobile.

The first wave of innovations and technology viability of engines proved that a two-wheeler automobile product was possible:

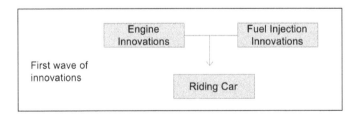

The second wave of engine and fuel injection innovations led to far wider range of vehicles:

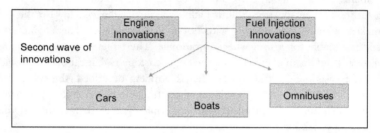

The second wave of innovations proved that there was a possibility of manufacturing four-wheel automobiles for the people who were travelling in horse-driven carriages. The market was available and the technology was viable. The problem/solution fit had been established. Now the product/market fit had to be explored. When the first cars were made, they were competing with the horse-driven carriages. They were trying to fill a gap that horse-driven carriages couldn't meet: speed and safety. When motor cabs replaced hand-driven horses, the emphasis was on how much roomier the motor cars were and how much safer they were when compared to horse-driven carriages. The following article clipping shows this pitch:

THE COMING OF THE MOTOR-CAB

A BEGINNING WILL BE MADE BY PLACING FIFTY OF THESE VEHICLES IN THE STREETS, AND ALREADY HUNDREDS OF DRIVERS ARE TAKING LESSONS IN CONTROLLING THE MOTOR-DRIVEN CAB

THE London public will soon have an opportunity of trying the motor-hansom. Experiments have been carried out for several months past by a company called the London Express Motor Service, Limited, which is placing fifty motor-driven hansom cabs on the streets a few weeks hence.

The prolonged trials with a specimen vehicle have proved that with certain modifications which have been adopted, motor - hansoms can be utilised to great advantage for the heavy work that metropolitan traffic entails. The dimensions of the motor-hansom, as may be judged from our photograph, are somewhat larger than those of the horse-drawn vehicle. There is more room inside, while in case of need an additional drop seat is fixed alongside the driver, who sits before the passengers, but somewhat lower and to one side, so that the view in front is not obstructed. The glass front has a spring attachment, and can be raised or lowered by the passengers. A distance indicator is placed inside the cab, so that there can be no dispute as to the actual distance travelled. Luggage can be carried in the boot at the rear of the body, and there is also room for luggage on the floor in front of the passengers and by the side of the driver. The chassis of the vehicles are being built in Paris, and the whole of the carriage work is being constructed by Messrs. Hy. Whitlock (Limited), Holland Gate, Kensington. The engines are twelve horse-power, double cylinder Astor governed, and slow running. The power is transmitted

THE MOTOR-HANSOM

through a Panhard type of gear to a Cardon driven axle. In order to eliminate any tendency to side-slip, the greater portion of the body has been constructed of aluminium to reduce the rear weight as much as possible. The engines are geared down to give greater hill-climbing power, and there are three speeds, the third giving about twenty-five miles an hour on the level.

It remains to be seen how the people will take to the new vehicles, but there can be no doubt as to the danger of travel in the existing hansom, chiefly due to the horse being so liable to fall on the slippery paving. The development of the new business will depend entirely upon the success attending the first twenty or so of the cabs placed upon the streets, but judging from the experience of the past six months' practical experiments, both as to working cost, and favour, there appears to be little doubt on this head. The policy of the company will then be to continue steadily to increase the number of motor-hansoms running ; it is anticipated that soon after they begin running there will be demands for at least five hundred. As the working cost is much below that of the horse-drawn cab, there appears to be no reason why the new cab should not gradually supplant the old method. The interest displayed by proprietors of cabs in the motor-driven cab points to this, while hundreds of drivers of the present hansoms have applied to be taught to drive the new motor-hansoms. These men are anxious to secure their new occupation before their old one is gone.

Source: https://en.wikipedia.org/wiki/History_of_the_automobile#/media/File:Motor-Hansom.jpg

So, what is the most impactful product?

As we saw from both the concepts of fail fast and mvp, there are gaps in how product teams apply these concepts to their context. In both cases, we seem to miss the part about "what do we want to learn?". We also seem to be missing the part about the unique business context that drives product goals. Applying fail fast and mvp as broad strokes, without underlying context, Key Business Outcomes, and market maturity isn't very smart. Both mvp and fail fast, I feel, are at the intersection of the 'what' and the 'how.' This can be useful for certain business scenarios, especially when in the problem/ solution fit stage. However, once technology viability and market needs are established, we cannot focus purely on viability and speed.

Looking again at the car makers history, having four wheels was always an integral part of the product that was competing to replace the horse-driven carriages. The earliest versions of the automobile had to offer something more than the horse-driven carriages were already offering, but they didn't have to have the same frills. The baseline on luxury was already set by the carriages. So, the minimum that even the first cars would need to have was defined by what a horse-driven carriage was offering. Whether the automobile could compete with horse-driven carriages could have been one of the riskiest propositions for the car makers. This was proven by the combustion engine's potential.

At this point, people adapting the engine-powered four-wheel automobiles were the early adopters. They were the folks who saw the immense potential of the automobile. They were the folks who were willing to forego frills to adapt this solution, because their need for speed and their concern with safety in horse-driven carriages far outweighed the lack of luxurious convenience. Bertha Benz was Carl Benz's wife. Without her husband's knowledge, she undertook a long trip with her two sons, proving that the four-wheeler, powered by the engine could sustain long drives. This was another proof of viability and it was seen as quite a sensation to have proved that automobiles had the potential to sustain long drives.

The first version of the car had to be already better than the horse and carriage. The subsequent versions of the car were iterations on the style, convenience, seating, and manufacturing processes. Between the late 19th century and the middle of the 20th century, car models had undergone significant improvements. As seen in the following images, the four-wheeler automobile spawned off so many variations in design, style, and features within the first 30-40 years after the first car went into production with an internal combustion engine. Car models continue to be launched, with electric cars and self-driving cars becoming popular now:

1885-built Benz Patent-Motorwagen, the first car to go into production with an internal combustion engine	The second Marcus car of 1888 at the Technical Museum in Vienna	The Ford highboy Coupe 1919

The innovations of Henry Ford (founder of the Ford Motor Company and a pioneer in the development of the assembly line technique of mass production) were in creating the assembly line. Manufacturing cars now had a viable cost proposition. Today's Tesla electric-powered cars were based on the viability of battery technology. An Impact Driven Product has one or more components of proven viability. However, the product cannot be impactful unless it appeals to the customer and can create a demand from the market that can help the business to grow, sustain, or influence.

Products for an unexplored market versus products for mature markets

There is a difference in how we should approach product building for an early stage business in a market where needs are not validated and where technology viability is not proven. In cases where a problem/solution fit is not established, mvp makes sense. In fact, in the problem/solution fit stage, sometimes, the mvp may not even be a product. It could be market research survey, concierge models of mvps, or a simple landing page with a promise of the product to come. After all, we are looking to test the unexplored market. Even there, we cannot blindly dive into building without thinking about the business outcomes and the target segment.

In established markets (where technology viability is proven or alternate business models exist) and in cases where we have validated the problem/solution fit, we need to expand our thinking beyond minimum viability. It's not about picking up the smallest scope of work. It is not about creating a prototype. It is not about blindly rushing to meet a timeline.

Businesses don't look at just one aspect of the product and assume that it will be successful. We need to look at the entire product experience, market needs, and commercial viability to create a product that is impactful. Impact is important not just at the early stages of product building but also in every subsequent phase. Product management needs to align about what is the smartest thing we can put together that can drive the most impact for our target customers.

What is our Impact Driven Product? We need to answer the following questions every time we enter the Impact Driven Product development cycle:

1. How do we grow as a business? What is the most impactful thing that will meet our Key Business Outcomes?

2. How do we deliver value to our customers? What is the unique differentiating product experience that will delight our customers?

3. Will our riskiest proposition nullify our biggest hypotheses? Will the failure of the product experience kill our business?

4. What is the smartest way to deliver impact? When, how, and by what means can we deliver impact? Smartest is not necessarily the smallest or fastest solution. Also, your idea of fast is not the same as my idea of fast. Speed is not about blindly racing toward a timeline, but looking at the timeline in the context of business impact and the internal and external constraints.

As indicated earlier, there are many factors that can impact when a product takes shape and is ready to be released:

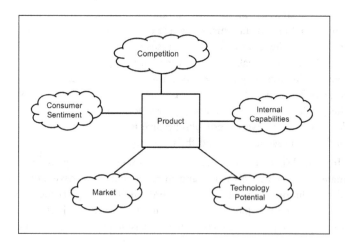

This statement from *The Innovator's Dilemma (Clayton M. Christensen)* captures this well: "When performance oversupply occurs, it creates an opportunity for a disruptive technology to emerge and subsequently invade established markets… the criteria by which customers will choose one product or service over another will change, signaling a transition from one phase to the next phase in the product life cycle."

By focusing on the minimum viability aspect of the product in a proven market, we are losing out on the opportunity to maximize the potential of a proven technology. Instead of aiming to create the utmost value for the customer and scripting the success for the business, are we limiting our thinking to creating the simplest possible product that will cushion our fall if we fail?

When we have validated that a market for four-wheeled automobiles exists, and if the technology viability has been proven, then we don't go and build a skateboard. We build the four-wheeled automobile that will delight our customers, even if it is a barebones, no frills version of the automobile. What we need to launch (even as the first version) is a product that is so valuable to the consumer that he or she will jump through hoops to adopt our product. We still need to identify early adopters in our target segment, but our first version of the product must be much broader than what we would define as a mvp today.

How do we know if we have defined the right Impact Driven Product?

Deciding upon a hypothesis about the product before we even begin product development is important. This hypothesis determines what we want to learn and should be centered around a specific target segment of consumers (you can't make everyone happy at the same time, so who do you want to choose first?). It needs to be based on a gap in the market or a critical need not addressed by any product today. You need to have the technological potential to close the gap or deliver the critical need to your target consumers. These are our prerequisites.

For instance, we could postulate that working women in urban Indian cities need safe travel options. So, let's say that business A is hypothesizing that women-driven cabs, that can be hailed with a mobile app and are personalized to women travelers, will be a successful product. However, is this a hypothesis backed by concrete evidence of what the consumer really wants? We see a gap in the market, a need that exists, but how do we know if an idea for a product meets what the consumer wants? What Key Business Outcomes will this product establish for business A?

Validate market needs based on Key Business Outcomes

Product building needs to be preceded by early validations with the customer base. These could be through conversations, research, or even a well-marketed landing page with options to sign up. Renault Duster's launch in India and its success in the SUV segment is worth recalling. Renault recognized a gap in the Indian car segment. SUVs manufactured by global players were in the Rs 20 lakh and above range. There was an opportunity to make SUVs in the under Rs 10 lakhs range. Renault was looking for volume drivers (http://www.businesstoday.in/magazine/case-study/case-study-renault-duster-success-story/story/199321.html). This was their key business outcome.

Learning from the failure of its earlier cars in India, Renault initiated a study for 200 people whose profile matched the potential buyer. Members of the product development team spent time with 30 of these families, to get to know what they liked and did not like about their vehicles.

The study revealed that rugged exterior looks, a chrome finish, dual tone interiors, and rear seating luxuries were important to their target group. Of course, the basic essentials of a car couldn't be compromised, but these aspects could tip the adoption of the SUV. Duster went on to capture 23% of the SUV market share within a year of its launch.

Now, it may have seemed counter-intuitive to think that Renault should have focused on chrome exteriors. Would the mvp version of the Duster have had this if Renault hadn't heard the consumer's view? Their riskiest proposition was how to differentiate their brand and create a volume driver. The company wasn't validating the idea of an SUV in the Indian market. For Renault, the operations, technology, and manufacturing viability had already been tested. However, for a new entrant in car manufacturing, the riskiest propositions would be many. The production team would have to validate many parallel aspects of the product, including the manufacturing, technology, positioning, and branding. Still, customers wouldn't adopt the car just because the new entrant managed to build the car against all odds. Customers don't care how we build our product. Customers care about the value our product creates for them.

This is where software businesses have a great advantage over traditional manufacturing industries. The entry barrier to creating a software product is so low. It is far easier (when compare to traditional marketing) to completely scrap a software product and rebuild it from scratch. It is so easy to create disruptive products with minimal investment. This is why Uber could so easily disrupt an existing ecosystem with a small team of engineers. So, we need to take advantage of that by ensuring that we are open to valuable feedback.

Validating if customers will adopt our product

Product adoption depends on the value that a product creates for the consumer. It boils down to how the product appeals to the emotional needs of a consumer. Is it taking away a pain or hurdle that the customer has today? Is it creating an aspirational state for the consumer? Does it look visually appealing? Does it make it harder for them to use the product when compared to their current alternative? Does it add more work than the current alternative? Is it available easily? It is a matter of pride to own this product?

We may choose to solve one and only one problem for the consumer: *a single end-to-end functional flow*. However, this functional flow needs to deliver the maximum impact to the consumer. If we're pioneering food delivery, then maybe it's alright to not have 100 cuisines on display, but it's not alright to deliver food gone cold. However, in a competitive food delivery market, not having ample choices on cuisines could be a disadvantage and delivering stale food is disastrous. So, we need to be wise in choosing what our mvp should be.

Design, branding, content, positioning, pricing, on-boarding experience, and usability need to work on top of the underlying technology to drive an unparalleled experience for the consumer. We can create the Most Valuable Product by focusing on the impact we want to drive. We may be feature poor, but we have to be experience rich. Remember product technology cannot work in isolation.

We could also discover new ways in which customers will use our product. I recall an experience narrated by a colleague in one of my previous workplaces. Her team had built a solar power solution that offered urban migrant settlers electricity. The solar charging device could power a light and a fan and charge their mobiles. The solution also had a great commercial model in which ultimately the migrants could own the solar power device. However, when the team had launched the solution, they realized that the migrants rarely used the device for lights or fans. They were used to living in those conditions and were habituated to complete their cooking and other chores before dusk. They instead procured low-end second-hand TVs and used the solar device to power the TV instead. The customer value the business predicted was quite different from the value that the customers saw in the solution. Validation and feedback is equally critical when designing Impact Driven Products.

What is the smartest way to deliver impact?

At a nonprofit organization, where I was leading the product team, we had started on a plan to redesign the fundraising platform. It was a web-based platform to crowdsource investments to help rural entrepreneurs. A significant number of investors were viewing our website on mobile. We weren't offering the best experience to them, since our fundraising platform was not mobile-ready. The website had been around for over 8 years, and had many functional flows and a lot of content. There were many options on the platform to invest or donate money to rural borrowers. We knew that a complete redesign of a feature-rich website was going to take forever. So, we planned an iterative approach. We identified the most visited pages on the website first using website analytics. The management stakeholder team had invested in fundraising as their Key Business Outcome. The combination of knowing which flows were frequently being used by our investors and which was the most important outcome for the organization gave us our most impactful part of the product.

We first launched a responsive version of the home page and a responsive version of our emailers. We then focused only on redesigning the core funding flow, chipping away at all the nonessential steps and reduced it to a two-step process. All other flows were not mobile friendly, but fixing this flow, coupled with the emailer content, ensured that when we sent monthly newsletters or payment reminders, our target group could read the email on their mobile and follow a link from there to our website's fully functional responsive funding flow. We could see a jump in our conversion rates and the number of investments increased quite significantly.

Now, this version of our platform was not exactly an mvp. We already had ample data to point us in the direction in which our target customers were headed. Being mobile ready was not something we had to test viability for. What we had to do was to craft the most impactful solution for our target segment. Again, redesigning the platform in isolation wasn't going help. We had to ensure that our end-to-end flow was geared for a mobile-first experience. Starting from the trigger of when the monthly reminders and newsletters were sent, leading on to the landing pages on the website, and following up with the core fundraising flow had to be orchestrated to ensure a seamless experience for the investors.

The limitations of a technology solution won't matter to the consumer. Even under the present limitations, can our product create value? Is there a market opportunity that can open up for a solution like this? If it does, then consumers will be willing to buy our product even with its limited functionality. Customers might be even willing to pay more for a solution that meets their needs.

The Innovator's Dilemma by *Clayton M. Christensen* explains why the 3.5-inch drive decisively conquered the desktop PC market. It talks about how computer makers had to pay on average 20% more per megabyte to use 3.5-inch drives and yet they flocked to use this drive instead of the 5.25-inch drive. This is because the capacity demand was met by the 3.25-inch drive, but a new demand was created now: the demand for smaller physical size. Once that was satiated, the next wave of demands around reliability and pricing came up.

Technology viability can open up opportunities and the potential for disruption, but market needs will drive competitiveness and differentiation. To respond swiftly to market needs, we need to exploit the flexibility that software development offers. We cannot assume that the market will appreciate the value of what we offer.

A product life cycle evolves based on how we respond to the inputs from the market. Every version of the product must address a non-negotiable core need of the market. Everything in the product must be about that core need. As the market need evolves (the consumer base expands or product adoption increases), the next wave of needs arises from the market. Products surf over waves of market demand until either the market demand reaches a tipping point or a drastic disruption in the market renders the product obsolete. Business intelligence is in, being able to watch out and prepare for those disruptions.

Iterate on scope

Going back to the case of ArtGalore, we need to evaluate the success criteria of the all the prioritized feature ideas. This will assist us to determine which of those will help us to create the most impactful product. Since we have already prioritized only the feature ideas which will have an impact on Key Business Outcomes, we can now focus on how to maximize the value to customers:

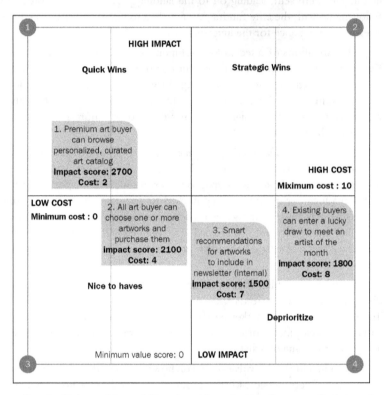

For ArtGalore, this could be about focusing on the ease of sign up for the art catalog, timing the newsletters (frequency, day of the month to publish, and so on), richness of content, ease in reaching out to the ArtGalore sales team for enquires based on what catches their eye in the newsletters, and so on. In case there is more than one feature idea, in the quick wins or strategic wins boxes, that needs to meet the same timelines/market-needs-driven milestones, we may have to slice through our success criteria to find the most impactful scope that we can deliver.

Needless to say, this is not a one-time activity that we do at launch. We need to follow through on how successful or not our efforts at maximizing customer value have been. So, we also need to set up channels for qualitative and quantitative feedback.

Happy customers at every phase of the product

Launching a product with more features than the market needs is wasteful. Early adopters will choose functionality over price, experience, and so on. To win early adopters, the product must meet their functional needs well. This helps us to build our product lean, but drive impact. However, a lean product is not necessarily a minimal product. So, my illustration for product development using the Impact Driven Product paradigm would be as follows:

The essential point is that the first version of an Impact Driven Product must be a complete product that not only works well but also is emotionally appealing and valuable enough for the customer to buy it and it meets business outcomes. It is surely not a skateboard. Each version of the product must be an Impact Driven Product based on the stage of market and business maturity. Ambitious thinking is crucial for building products.

Summary

Understanding business outcomes, market needs, customer value, technology viability, and competitive advantage is necessary to craft the right kind of product experience. Knowing the intent of what our product seeks to validate, or accomplish, is a necessary first step. Understanding the pulse of the market and a customer's needs is important for knowing what works well and how our customers perceive the value of our product.

Now that we have defined the right approach for deciding between managing scope, MVP, and the Impact Driven Product, let's find out in the next chapter how qualitative and quantitative customer feedback can influence product direction.

7

TRACK, MEASURE, AND REVIEW CUSTOMER FEEDBACK

Exploring customer perspectives and context can help us uncover new opportunities. We may build a technologically superior and robust product, but that alone cannot guarantee that our product will succeed. Product success can depend on how customers adopt our product, how they perceive our product's value, and the alternatives that exist in the market among other things. We cannot predict how products will be received by our customers. Customers may adopt our product in ways we didn't expect them to. By keeping an ear to the ground and a check on the pulse of the market, we can tweak our product experience to identify new value propositions in our Impact Driven Product.

In this chapter, we will explore the following topics:

* Why do well-made products fail?
* Categorizing customers by level of engagement
* Feedback channels and when to use them
* Incorporating feedback into the product backlog

Why do well-made products fail?

> *"What's really going to bake your noodle later on is,*
> *would you still have broken it if I hadn't said anything?"*
> *– Oracle, The Matrix*

Charles Duhigg, in the book, *The Power of Habits,* explores the launch of Febreze, its initial failure, and how understanding customer context and motivations made it a success. The following is a summary of the case study described in the book.

Procter & Gamble (P&G), a corporate behemoth with a wide range of household products had an interesting experience launching Febreze. It was an innovative product that could eradicate bad odor. It was inexpensive to manufacture, and it could be sprayed on fabrics in homes and car interiors.

The product was so phenomenal in eliminating odor that the team was very confident about its success in the market. The marketing team created ad campaigns using the cues, routine, and reward framework of the habit loop, that Charles Duhigg explains in his book. The cue was an everyday situation where we encounter bad odor. The routine (the team hoped) was to spray Febreze. The reward was eliminating bad odor:

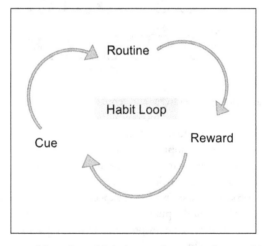

P&G was confident that with its innovative technology and its ubiquitous need in regular households, Febreze was going to be a hit. After the launch, the company waited for a week, two weeks, a month, and two months. Febreze sales hadn't taken off at all. It was a failure. The entire team was confounded. It seemed to them that they had done everything right. The product was effective, it was easy to manufacture, they had their distribution channels in place, the ads were well made, the launch was perfect, and there was a clear need for such a product in the market. What was going on, then? Didn't people want to eliminate odor? Their initial market research interviews had revealed compelling data that people wanted to eliminate odors, not just mask them, so then why didn't Febreze take off as expected?

Understanding customer context

P&G started to investigate. It interacted with and observed people's household cleaning routines. That is when the team hit upon their first observation that challenged a fundamental assumption they had made about how people perceive harsh odors in their houses. They realized that we become desensitized to the smells in our lives. If you're a cigarette smoker, then you don't smell smoke after a while. As Charles Duhigg observes in the book, even the strongest odors fade with constant exposure. The **cue** of the habit loop wasn't kicking in, since people were unaware of the bad odor.

The second key insight came when they also noticed how consumers used Febreze. They were using it as a finishing touch *after* their regular cleaning routine. One of the customers they interviewed observed, "spraying feels like a little mini-celebration when I'm done with a room." Febreze was not a part of the cleaning **routine**, instead it was the **reward** at the end of the cleaning routine.

P&G now had a tangible solution to their problem. The product was great, but it was the positioning and its value to the customer in relation to their context that had to be changed. Their ads now advertised Febreze as a reward at the end of the cleaning routine, and they also added perfume to the product, to emphasize that Febreze was a prize for cleaning efforts. A year later, Febreze brought in $230 million."(Source: *The Power of Habit*, *Charles Duhigg* – http://charlesduhigg.com/new-york-times-magazine/.)

An instance of product adoption and its relation to human behavior, can be found in Malcolm Gladwell's *Tipping Point*. A study was conducted in the '60s about the importance of fear in learning. One group of participants was taught about the importance of tetanus inoculation. Another group was given a booklet with the dangers of tetanus. A camp for getting the tetanus shot was set up. Surprisingly, even though the latter group said they were more likely to get the tetanus shots (after reading the booklet), almost none of the participants from either group actually got their tetanus shots. Neither fear nor education had been effective in nudging the participants to take action. In a repeat of this experiment, the team included a map of the local area showing where they could get tetanus shots. This was given to both groups. A large number of participants from both groups got their tetanus shots this time. Where fear and education had failed, a simple map succeeded (source: *The Tipping Point, Malcom Gladwell* – https://www.litcharts.com/lit/the-tipping-point/chapter-three-the-stickiness-factor).

These amazing stories from P&G and from the tetanus shot study, tell us a lot about why product adoption isn't straightforward and well-defined. If we asked people why they didn't take the tetanus shots, we would have received a lot of explanations, none of which could have pointed us to the solution of showing a simple map. We cannot guess the context under which our product is being used by our consumers. Looking purely at data, without its context, may not really help in improving our product experience.

Feedback doesn't always come wrapped in nice packages. It is usually never clear, specific, or constructive. It never tells us what action to take. Unearthing product insights is only possible when we understand the context under which consumers use our product. That is, if we get feedback at all to begin with.

The purpose of seeking feedback is to help us assess whether the assumptions we have made about our product hold true or not. In the case of Febreze, the assumption was that the product would become an integral part of the cleaning routine. What the consumer context told the team was that it was a reward at the end of the regular cleaning routine. It also gave them the valuable insight about people being nose blind when it comes to smells in their lives. If they hadn't gone to the core of the consumer context, the P&G team could have continued to make improvements to the product, without changing their fundamental assumptions. They would have made many more enhancements to try to make people adopt Febreze as part of their cleaning routine, and each attempt would have hit a roadblock because people were unaware of odor problems, and they weren't really looking to change their cleaning routines.

Feedback blind spots

We can be blindsided about how we seek product feedback. The first blind spot, as we saw, is being unaware of our underlying assumptions. This was described in the examples of Febreze and the tetanus shots. Even when focusing on the right business outcomes and customer value, and having done the necessary market analysis alongside having the technology viability, our core assumptions about how customers will perceive our product can be flawed.

The second blind spot is that of seeking feedback only from the customers that contribute to our success. Focusing only on what works well without trying to explore why our product doesn't work well for other target segments or certain cohorts within our target segments, can lead to biased insights. Both these blind spots require that we get out of the building, talk to our customers, and resist ideating only based on our existing biases and mental models.

Product feedback is sometimes less about what is being said and more about what we're not hearing. We miss out on the silent/indifferent customers: the ones who don't feel empowered to offer feedback and who are indifferent to our product. This could happen to all of us because of our unconscious biases. Creating formal or informal channels for engaging the silent consumer can be quite valuable. Later in this chapter, we will explore some ways to gather feedback.

> *"Ten thousand people, maybe more*
>
> *People talking without speaking*
>
> *People hearing without listening*
>
> *People writing songs that voices never share*
>
> *And no one dared*
>
> *Disturb the sound of silence."*
>
> — *The Sound of Silence, Simon & Garfunkel*

So, what do we mean by silent customers? Let me narrate an incident. Residential apartment complexes in Bengaluru, India, have to constitute managing committees to oversee the apartment facilities, maintenance, and services. The committee is formed by people residing in the apartment complexes. While the residents oversee the overall maintenance, usually there is an estate manager or a supervisor who runs the day-to-day affairs in terms of housekeeping and other services.

A few years ago, I was part of my apartment's managing committee. A few weeks after joining the committee, I had gone down to inspect the housekeeping women's facilities. I realized that their changing rooms were in an appalling condition. I was quite shocked that the lock on the door was broken, there were no curtains for the one open point of ventilation, and even the tap was broken. Even more shocking was that this was how things had been for over a year. So, why hadn't anyone fixed these issues?

The housekeeping team worked under the supervision of the estate manager and a housekeeping supervisor, who were both men. To expect that the women would even talk to the men about their changing room facilities was not practical. Fortunately, they didn't have that inhibition with me. They were willing to openly discuss their problems.

Eventually, it took us only a day to fix the changing rooms. Everyone, including the estate manager and the supervisor, was willing to solve the problem. They never knew that these problems existed in the first place. The housekeeping women are akin to silent consumers. We hadn't created channels to engage and hear from them. This type of disconnect may also exist between certain groups of users and businesses. If we lead ourselves into believing that no news is good news, then we have lost a great opportunity to unlock product potential.

Types of customers

Not every customer is a silent customer, nor is every customer vocal in sharing valuable feedback about our product. Customers will continue to put up with a lot of discomfort, up until the time that they can find a better alternative. We could be completely in the dark about this, because the customers never spoke up or because we didn't make an effort to reach out to them. In a competitive business landscape, finding the differentiating value that will ensure that our users stay loyal to our product, even if they have to bear with a broken or incomplete product experience must remain the top priority. Product experience could mean everything from marketing, sales, ease of access, ease of purchasing, product support, ease of use, and so on. Based on how customers value the product or solution (how well it solves their problems / meets their needs / is desirable and the availability of other alternatives) and based on what their overall product experience is (support, service, accessibility, pricing, and so on), we can categorize customers, as shown in the following illustration:

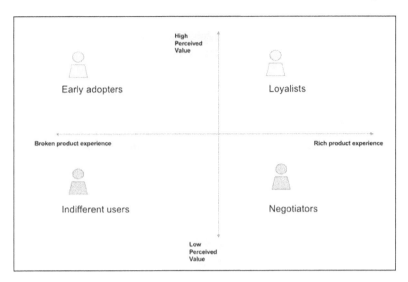

Early adopters are the customers who are willing to jump through hoops to use our product, because our product offers them a very valuable solution to their pressing problem. They will not mind a broken product experience, as long as the product delivers value. Loyalists are the customers who swear by the product value. The product experience keeps them locked in. The product meets their core needs, meets their price point, and in general, offers an end-to-end experience that the customer feels great about. Also, the alternatives in the market may not measure up to our product's value or experience or the cost of switching could be higher.

The negotiators may have no incentive to adopt our product or they may be in a position to find many alternatives to our solution. So, they perceive our product's value to be low. They find every opportunity to negotiate in order to compensate for the perceived lack of value by negotiating on price and requesting additional support, discounts, or freebies in order to use our product. The indifferent users and the silent users are forced to use the product for lack of viable alternatives or for not having a say in product selection. This could happen when the paying customer is different from the actual user of the solution.

All four categories of customers will be ready to switch to an alternate competitive product/solution when such an option is available. The loyalists may take longer to switch, but eventually if the market is moving toward a new alternative, they will follow suit.

An alternative solution that offers better value will always be attractive. What may prevent users from discontinuing using our product is the high costs of switching products. This could be in terms of the commercials of switching, locked in data, and so on. However, if the value provided by the alternative product supersedes the costs of switching, then there will be little hesitation from a customer who wants to switch. Product experience must ensure that consumers stay locked in, even when alternatives exist in the market that offer the same or a higher value.

Naturally, businesses want to lock users into the loyalty box. The investment we make in seeking product feedback should enable us to gain insights that can help to scale up value, gain an edge over the competition, and improve the product experience:

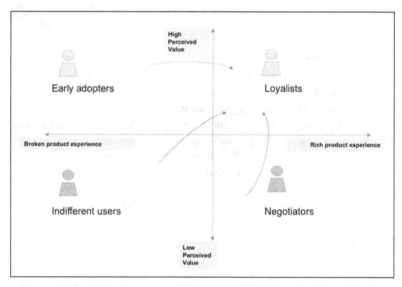

Our efforts when seeking feedback should help us assess these two aspects:

- What is the perceived value of our product? How well does our product meet customer needs when compared to existing alternatives? Is there a problem/solution fit?
- What aspect of our product experience matters to our customers? How much of a broken product experience are our customers willing to put up with to continue to use our product?

Understanding the perceived value of our product

We set the course for the direction that we want our product to take by investing in Key Business Outcomes and deriving impact scores. Our Impact Driven Product may still have some assumptions we made about why our product will succeed. However, we're still making these assumptions in the blind. Even when we have ample data from customer interviews and our study of the market and have a good hold on what the market needs, the real data only comes if the market actually adopts our product in the way that we assumed it would. How our users perceive the value of our product may or may not match our intended value. We need to look out for the evidence that points us to anything that challenges our assumptions about the product. However, if we look only for confirmation of our assumptions, the chances are that we will always find it. Confirmation bias will ensure that we continue to read only the signals that will reinforce our existing beliefs.

This is a problem because it will take us much longer to realize that our product is a failure, and we may have lost precious time and opportunity to course correct. It also means that we may lose out on finding new purposes that customers might be using our product for, in ways that we didn't anticipate. We may lose an opportunity to discover customers who use our product for problems that we didn't intend to solve. In the previous chapter, we read about how the urban migrant settlers used the solar power devices for powering their TVs, rather than using them for basic lighting needs. This is a good case in point about customers using our solutions in ways that we didn't intend.

So, in essence, *perceived value – proposed value = business opportunity*.

The proposed value is the value that a business attaches to the impact their product creates for the target customer. The perceived value is the value that the customer attaches to the product. In both cases, the value is a combination of how well the product meets customers' needs and solves their problems, and how satisfying the product experience is.

The difference between these two values can indicate the business opportunity/potential. When the business values its product more than the consumers does, it stands to lose out to its competition because customer retention and loyalty drops. However, when consumers value a product more than the business or use the product in ways not anticipated, it opens up opportunities to increase revenue and market share, and also for new business models/products.

A case in point is how the company CommonFloor pivoted its business model. CommonFloor launched as an apartment community management solution in India. The initial intent was to create a forum for apartment residents to be able to communicate, share, and interact with each other. However, when the founding team analyzed the nature of the posts and interactions between community members on forums of all the apartments they had on-boarded, they discovered something unique and interesting. They observed that many of the postings on the open forum were around the buying/selling or renting properties.

The founders realized the potential that their platform held. They had uncovered a new opportunity and an unmet need of their customers. People didn't have an easy way to post rental listings online. This realization was what led to the re-imagination of the platform as a real estate listing portal.

Quoting Lalit Mangal, the then CTO and cofounder of CommonFloor (which is now acquired by Quikr) from a published article: "In the initial years, we noticed a lot of home owners had started using our platform to post listings. We realized that it would add much more value to the owners if we opened this information to people outside the gated communities. We started project listing on our site. When we noticed that the traffic on our website increased, we started verifying the listed properties. Soon, we were recognized as the best place for genuine listings and started seeing a lot of traction from those looking to buy/sell or rent a house." (`http://emavericks. in/wp-content/uploads/2015/11/eMavericks-Insight-Volume-1-Issue-3.pdf`.)

Success metrics, that we defined as part of our features, are a great place to look for indicators that tell us how close or far we are from our success goals. The number of leads, customer retention rates, new customers gained, profits, revenue, and so on are tangible measurable matrices. However, taking the numbers at face value and not understanding the rationale behind those numbers is not a great move.

Let's assume that we had a success goal of gaining 500 new customers in the 3 months after our launch. What happens when we don't meet that goal? The response that most of us have when we see numbers that don't meet our success criteria is to blame the first, most convenient event. We might say, "The website outage might have been the reason. The emailers didn't go on time. We don't have a dedicated support team." This is attribution bias: we surmise that a one-off event caused our failure or that we didn't try hard enough. Yet, with an invigorating pep-talk, and a grand vision laid out, we could all do better this time. We re-establish our goals and set off on the same mission without changing a thing in our product. Our conviction that our product is great, and the failure is only due to some external factor or bad luck is sure to set us back on finding the right reasons that caused our product to fail. Openness to feedback, a willingness to go beyond looking at numbers at face value, and uncovering the customer context that could influence the success/failure of our product, is essential for product management.

Even among the customer segment that purchased our product, we need to explore how well they use our product. Are there parts of our product that are used more often than the others? How often do our customers seek help from us? How many customer complaints do we receive? What nature of complaints do we receive? Is there a certain type of user or a certain demography that uses our product more frequently than others?

Product managers must continue to keep alive the idea of exploratory feedback loops. We need to ask the questions that we didn't anticipate before building the product. We need the ability to look for clues and patterns in the existing metrics we have. We need to find ways to discover the silent/indifferent customers and engage with them. We also can assess what new functionality to introduce in our product. Do customers feel a that lack of functionality is limiting their use of the product? Is there a new feature that customers are willing to pay more for? Each feature should go through a problem/solution fit validation.

Some of these actions can be carried out by just playing around with product pricing. We can assess how much more customers are willing to pay for a new feature. We could propose different plans and feature bundles to different sets of customers and validate which feature bundle works well. The most fundamental questions are: if we increase the price of the product by introducing this new feature, how will it affect our acquisitions and retentions? If we remove this product feature without decreasing the price, are we losing customers?

What aspect of our product experience matters most?

Product experience includes all the supporting aspects of the core product. This includes pricing, support, content, channels, marketing, sales, and so on. Customers' perceived value also includes the aspects of the end-to-end product experience. Are customers willing to put up with a lack of adequate support at a given price point? What barriers to adoption do they face with our product? What stops them from switching to an alternative solution?

In my own start-up, the mobile app platform for conferences and events, we were always looking for ideas to engage the conference audience. We had just introduced a quiz as part of our mobile app platform. Our bet was that people would love the game, and it would boost engagement. This turned out to be true. The engagement spike and the usage of the quiz was indeed great. Our customers were also willing to pay more for such a feature.

The event organizing companies (who were our customers) had a dedicated team that took care of the event logistics and audience engagement. They had been doing this manually, without using any digital tools. The idea of the mobile app was lucrative to them, because their customers (the event sponsors) and the event audience wanted innovative, digital interactions. Some of these conferences were held once every year, and the event organizers were always looking to try out something new every year.

Our quiz feature got quite a few of our customers excited. However, what we realized was that the success of the feature was dependent on the event managers who were on the ground during the event. While our platform offered a framework for creating and running a quiz, and well-designed leaderboards, the actual quiz questions had to be set up by the event team, based on the theme and target audience for each event. So, the success or failure of this feature was dependent on whether or not the event managers could spare the time to prepare the content for these quizzes. Were they willing to put in the work needed to not just create the content for the quiz but also to popularize it among the audience?

Event managers had very little time at their disposal, especially during the lead up to the event. They had to attend to a lot of last-minute details. The quiz added one more thing to their ever-growing list of things to do. While the value of our quiz app was high, the demand in terms of time and effort to effectively utilize the quiz was also high.

We realized that the event organizers who successfully used the quiz feature were the ones that had a bigger team at their disposal, or they had always run games and quizzes in their events. So, they were already in the habit of preparing the content for the games and quizzes. Our app saved time for them by consolidating and displaying results without any additional effort from their end. Our app had solved the results consolidation problem and not really the engagement/content creation problem.

However, for other event organizers, the quiz feature gave them a good value proposition to take to their customers, but it also demanded a lot of effort and time from them. Their inclination to adopt was quite low. These event organizers almost always reached out to us to see if we could help them with setting up the quiz, uploading the questions, and so on. These customers were negotiators. All these customers were willing to pay more for a feature like the quiz, but the expectation of support was higher from the negotiator group. They were always willing to switch to any alternative that could solve the problem of setting up quiz questions for them on demand. This presented an opportunity for us.

Whether we choose to act on an opportunity is a decision based on what Key Business Outcomes matter to us. It is possible that a competitor can learn from the barriers of adoption in our product and beat us to grab this opportunity.

"The early bird gets the worm, but it's the second mouse that gets the cheese."

– Unknown

Consumers care very little about how hard we worked to build our product or whether we're the first in the market or not. They care about the value, the urgency of the need for a solution to their problem, the ease of access to the product, pricing and access to support, among other things. When a market is saturated with many alternatives, with minor variations in features, and all priced more or less equally, branding recall, and product experience may become an important factor in choosing a product. Discounts, value-added services, switching costs, and locked-in value might also impact the decision of choosing an alternative product.

However, when there are no viable alternatives, and when the cost of switching is negligible, our product can get away with offering a broken product experience. A new company can now copy our product's core propositions and offer a rich product experience and attract our consumer base. Testing the limits of a consumer's tolerance of poor product experience cannot be a long-term strategy. Sooner or later the competition will catch up and beat us with a better experience, higher value proposition, or a better business model.

Creating product loyalists

Once the product value has been validated, improving the product experience can move the early adopters, negotiators, and silent customers into loyalists. For instance, the stickiness created by placing a visual map of the place to get the tetanus shot was purely an improvement of product experience. The value of the tetanus shot was clear, but the product experience was broken. Fixing that converted the indifferent students who came over to get tetanus shots.

Again, I recall an incident from my start-up days. We were seeing steady interest from medical conference organizers were keen on adopting our apps. However, the doctors who chaired the conference committees always had a busy schedule. Our initial (and rather novice) sales approach was to meet them in person. We would take a demo app on our phone and showcase the capabilities to them. We would hand our business cards to them and wait for them to respond, but we never usually heard back. We would continue to follow up multiple times, and in some rare occasions, would get a response asking us to call them later.

Now, we knew that they were quite impressed with our product and the pricing we were offering them. Yet, there was something that was blocking the conversion of sales. It was not sustainable for us to keep travelling to meet these doctors, given Bengaluru traffic conditions and the rather unpredictable schedules of these doctors. We realized that because the doctors had such hectic schedules, they were quite unlikely to remember us. Our business cards weren't enough to remind them about our app or its value proposition. Unlike our other customers (mainstream event organizers), not all doctors had the time or inclination to search for our website and learn about us online.

After all, many of the doctors were used to reading through paper files of medical records. Meeting a few such doctors helped us to understand the missing link in our product's sales experience. We realized that we needed to leave behind printed materials that they could read up on when they had the time. We solved the problem by printing brochures with high-quality images and app features clearly laid out. We started to leave behind printed brochures with the doctors. While this was not something that necessarily clinched many deals for us, it surely helped to create a better brand recall for us. It was an inexpensive and simple improvement. It worked better than leaving behind our business cards. On one occasion, I observed a doctor sharing our product brochure with another colleague. He was able to explain the value of our app and was literally doing our job for us! We had converted a silent lead into an influencer.

Knowing who the real user is

Optimizing product value proposition and experience based on feedback is great, but it is effective only when we seek feedback from the right customers. Valuable feedback from the wrong user can be quite ineffective. In fact, failing to understand the primary users of the product can cause a significant rework.

During my tenure working at a software consultancy, we had built a solution for the C-level team of a large corporate. We defined the persona of the typical C-level executive. We knew that the users were spread across the globe. We knew they would be travelling a lot. So, we spent a lot of time trying to optimize our product to address the needs of a person with little time on their hands, who needed access to information (mostly confidential reports) on the go.

This was many years ago, and at a time when mobile apps were not even around. The product development kept getting delayed, as we continued to optimize our experience for these users. We were quite iterative in our approach and had regular showcases with client stakeholders too. We seemed to be headed the right direction, and we weren't expecting any major surprises after launch.

However, after our launch, we kept receiving requests and complaints that certain parts of the report were not printing out well. We were amused, and very curious as to why the reports were even being printed. Why would a C-level executive print out a report when we expected them to just access the app on their laptops? We wondered if there was some aspect of security or confidentiality that was being compromised.

When we explored further, we discovered that nearly everyone in the C-level team had executive assistants. The assistants took care of most of the app usage on behalf of the C-level executives. The assistants would use the app to pull out the reports, print them, and then hand them to the C-level executives. Most of the C-level team nearly never used the app themselves.

Executive assistants weren't even in our target personas. The client stakeholders hadn't thought it was important to design the app for the people who were going to be the primary users of the app. Since it was an app for internal usage, the stakeholders had tried to design the best solution for the powerful folks in their organization. The actual users were now forced to use a solution in which they had had no say. This is another instance of silent/indifferent customers. However, once we got to know this, we acted swiftly to redesign our product experience to meet the primary user's needs.

We shouldn't ideally have to wait until after a product launches to gather this type of insight. What can be discovered during the product ideation can be way more powerful in delivering value, with little scope for a rework. Insights of this nature indicate a lack of understanding of the consumer's context. When we lack opportunities to gain consumer context, product development proceeds based on broad assumptions about the users, and about our value proposition to them.

In my example. the riskiest assumptions, and a large part of our efforts, were based on the core assumption that the C-level team were the primary users, and everything centered around that assumption. The product feedback cycle unearthed evidence that completely thwarted this belief. The goal for an Impact Driven Product team should be to shorten the Build-Measure-Learn loop, and learn fast and iterate on the value that we can offer in the product functionality and product experience.

How and when to collect feedback?

Feedback collection cannot be kicked off only when we hit a problem, such as if we see a volley of complaints and someone higher up tells us to find out what's going on. We explore possible interaction analytics that can be hooked up. We explore feedback collection tools. We even send out surveys. We clamor for a conversation with consumers and so on. This, needless to say, is the most ineffective way to approach product feedback. We must consider every opportunity to understand how consumers perceive our product. There are two aspects to this:

- What external channels can we leverage to gain these insights?
- What feedback channels can we build within the product?

External feedback channels

Sales and customer support are both essential channels to engage a consumer. Product teams must make it a part of their routine process to drive sales and support conversations. The following are some techniques we can use to understand customer feedback through channels external to the product itself:

1. Social media sentiment is a great indicator of understanding about what consumers are saying about our product. While influencers may be somewhat overrated in driving loyalty, there have also been instances where an influencer's actions or social comments have brought significant financial losses to brands. For instance, Kylie Jenner's tweet on her disappointment about Snapchat's redesign, cost Snapchat $1.3 billion (https://techcrunch.com/2018/01/11/snapchat-redesign-uninstall/).

2. Exploring the competition's value proposition, is also another input that can feed into our product feedback.

3. A/B testing with content, messaging, and pricing on the product website / marketing content / targeted user groups can help us to understand how customers perceive product value.

4. Creating channels to engage the consumer through conversations can be beneficial. In-person conversations, especially in the case of B2B products, can help to uncover contextual information about the customer's organization. We should explore opportunities to observe how consumers use our product, and the context setting under which they use the product. Our mental model as a product developer can be very different from that of the end user. Even a silent observation of how the actual user interacts with our product can be quite an eye-opener. The in-person sales interactions for medical conferences were an important forum for understanding the context of the doctors.

5. Getting out of the building. This is not just a product manager's or the founding team's responsibility. Every person on the product team must try to sell the product, market the product, demo the product, support a product complaint, and try to speak to as many customers as possible. The impact of such first-hand interactions with users of our product is invaluable.

6. Sales and revenue numbers are an important source of product feedback. A drop in retention rates, drop in sales, drop in subscription renewals, or even active cancellations and so on can unearth why the perceived value of our product is changing.

In-built feedback channels

Our product itself can have in-built options to capture user interaction metrics:

1. User interaction analytics on core functional flows can tell us where consumers drop off and how long they spend at each stage of our product workflow. We can use heat maps of product usage, active usage times (peaks/troughs), and so on.

2. Include feedback rating/questionnaires as part of core user flows.

3. Making support/help accessible and visible in our product flow can also help. Being present for support when a consumer is facing a block can unearth a great deal about the user's context.

4. Capture referrals from existing customers. Word of mouth or referrals are a great way to assess how well we perform on product loyalty.

Is the consumer ready to share feedback?

We have come to place so much emphasis on data and patterns. While data from a large number of folks can tell us a great deal, it cannot tell us everything. Large datasets lack individual context. The general assumption we make about product feedback is that we need to approach specific people and ask for specific information. Keeping our ears to the ground and getting a bird's eye view of the landscape are both equally important.

When it comes to product feedback, we tend to focus on creating star ratings or a low barrier form. We prefer close-ended questions rather than open comments such as: how would you rate our service? What can we improve about our website? Would you recommend us to a friend?

The missing link I see with this approach is that it helps in confirming our existing assumptions, rather than giving us new insights. It can give us a general health check or a pulse of the consumer sentiment, but doesn't usually add any other value. I almost always give a four- or five-star rating in every feedback form. This is not because I was wowed by the product or service, but because I don't want to answer a follow-through comment box that pops up if I rated anything less than three. I really don't have the inclination to comment.

So, even when, say, an e-commerce brand forces a feedback form on the segment like me (who belong to the largely indifferent/silent customer group) the responses they get may not be reflective of the underlying indifference. The indifferent consumer may not even report small lags in product experience. The broken product experience may add to the indifference, but it is not enough to push the indifferent consumer into even making a product complaint.

If the product service is really bad and may cost the consumer money, or a loss of data, or an infringement on privacy, then the indifferent/silent consumer will speak up. Unfortunately, that is exactly when businesses make it harder for us to reach their customer support. Support lines put you on hold, you have to replay your experience to seven different support assistants, and so on. Yet you receive no follow up calls and so on. The influential, but so far indifferent, consumer can then resort to an outrage on social media and cause damage to the brand image.

The threshold of tolerance for the broken product experience depends on existing alternatives and switching costs. I have often heard product teams come up with a diktat that we should always ask for minimal information from our consumers. It is harder for us to automatically process open comments. So, we choose close-ended questions and to-the-point, short feedback forms, that can give us data which can be sliced and diced. This is because we assume that consumers don't have the time to write down feedback. We feel that consumers are doing us a favor by giving us feedback. We cannot infringe on their time. We have to ask for minimal information. We have to ask for it at the right moment, and, if needed, we have to offer them incentives to share information with us. So, is this always true?

In a B2C market offering a low-cost, fast-moving product, saturated with competing products, and with very low switching costs, the consumer is spoilt for choice. The tolerance for a broken product experience can be very low. Retail e-commerce apparel websites in India, for instance, are dime a dozen and switching costs are nonexistent. Pretty much every brand offers the same experience, so loyalty is also nearly nonexistent. Asking your consumers for even a small bit of information, or to take an extra step without demonstrating a value, or offering a cookie in return, will be futile.

However, this strategy isn't necessarily true for a legal firm offering niche consulting services in corporate legal affairs. A B2B offering, like this, might require even potential leads to fill out detailed forms, and offer much more information and face-to-face meetings before they are even considered a qualified lead. The value offered by the legal consulting firm is very high. The chances of finding an alternative in that niche space could be much lower. Conversion cycles would be much longer and could run into months. Both parties, the firm and the corporate, would have to engage in a much higher level of information exchange before they close the deal.

The amount of effort put in by both parties itself makes it so much harder for the parties to break the deal. There is a lot at stake. Unless there is a significant breach of trust, switching costs would be too high, and would be a deterrent. In such cases, feedback cannot be a star rating form! There is no risk in asking for detailed information or having a personalized conversation about feedback and customizing the experience. This will be perceived as a value, rather than an intrusion. So, we need to understand the position of our product in the market, available alternatives, the perceived value of our product in the eyes of the consumer, switching costs, and so on.

Let's not take a generic, run-of-the-mill approach, without business or market context. Some aspects to definitely consider when asking for any information from the customer are as follows:

- What is the best channel to get information – online/offline/ personal face-to-face/phone, and so on?
- When is the best time to seek this information?
- Who are the most effective user groups to reach out to and seek inputs from?

Also, standard data analysis must be built into the product, and not left for the interpersonal feedback process to fill in. Demographic data (profile, region, and language), usage patterns (peaks, buying patterns, and frequent uses), drop off rates, retention rates, and so on, can easily be captured. They should serve as supplementary information that can help us to arrive at the root cause for an insight that we have gathered from a deeper consumer feedback.

The data can also potentially expose gaps. We may be able to find that we receive feedback from a certain segment of our customers. Other cohorts may not be sharing feedback with us. The same can be said for customer complaints. We need to look not just at the data we have but also take a step back and look at who is missing in our feedback data. This, once again, could present an opportunity for us to improve our product experience or product functionality, but only if we manage to discover and engage the silent customers:

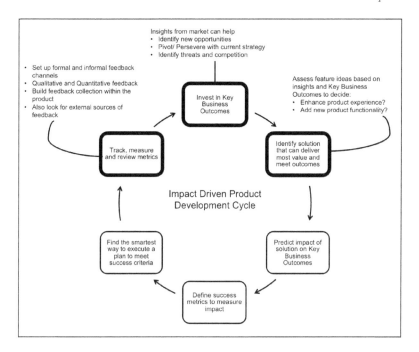

Summary

Product success depends on so many factors. The insights we get from tracking, measuring, and reviewing quantitative and qualitative metrics, through formal and informal channels, must help us to make informed decisions about our product strategy. This can help us to position our product better in terms of pricing and brand value. It can also help us to identify new opportunities too. Product feedback can be an important lever that drives the investment in Key Business Outcomes for the Impact Driven Product.

In this chapter, we completed an end-to-end lifecycle for a new feature idea. We measured product value from a customer's perspective. In the next chapter, we can deep dive into measuring short-term and long term product performance in terms of investments we made in Key Business Outcomes.

8

TRACKING OUR PROGRESS

"Nobody panics when things go according to plan,
even if the plan is horrifying."

– The Joker, The Dark Knight

The success of a product strategy depends on various factors. When operating under ambiguity, data and metrics can help to us steer the product in the right direction, but knowing what metrics to capture and when to use them, is also important. Looking at micro-level, short-term indicators alone cannot tell us how to steer our product in the ambiguous business ecosystem. Product management must be able to take an in-depth, detailed view of feature-level performance metrics. At the same time, they must be able to step back and take a bird's eye view of the larger landscape and see how product strategy must be shaped based on macro-level indicators.

The need for gratification

Instant gratification can be same-day deliveries, self-checkout lanes, superfast streaming speeds, instant cab hailing at our fingertips, and so many more services, which have created in us an inability to wait. "I want it, and I want it now," has become the default stance of the consumer today. A study by Associate Professor Ramesh Sitaraman and collaborators at Akamai demonstrated that viewers begin to abandon a site if the video does not start up within two seconds. Beyond two seconds, every additional one-second delay resulted in roughly a 5.8% increase in the abandonment rate (`https://www.cics.umass.edu/news/latest-news/research-online-videos`).

The need for instant gratification has influenced not only how products and services are built but also our ability to think about long-terms goals. The hard part for us to reconcile is that overnight successes took decades in the making. Speed is paramount in an ever-changing business landscape and to navigate this ambiguity, we set short-term goals and we measure our success by the day. Key Performance Indicators and product metrics revolve around meeting the hourly, daily, and weekly numbers, but there is only so much we can learn from short-term metrics.

Product strategy is hard to formulate without a longer-term view. In the context of this long-term view, we need to take informed decisions about where we are willing to take a hit in order to make a longer-term impact. We can't strategize for the short-term and hope to succeed in the long term. Yet nearly all the messages we get from the world tell us to celebrate visible, quick success. The need for speed, quicker to market capabilities, and to pivot, persevere, or perish all seem to revolve around our ability to read market signals and respond really fast. If we don't read the market signals, we will fall behind. If we don't deliver on time, someone else will beat us to the market.

These are all true statements. All the fine-grained details of product performance do matter. Speed matters. We need to be meticulous about gathering data around our success metrics and gather them fast. How we interpret that data, and how that data affects our strategy, is what will differentiate us. This will define the unique nature of our business. Getting excited at the first positive sign and thinking about a pivot at the first downside isn't going to help.

Product metrics is only one dimension of data that will help to evaluate our performance. While the speed of delivery is crucial, the same cannot be said about the speed of interpreting product metrics. We already addressed one aspect of this problem when we defined success metrics. Taking into consideration the realistically achievable successes and making them reasonably time-bound can tell us whether our product feature is working well or not. However, that doesn't necessarily tell us if the product strategy is working well.

Product strategy needs a much longer period of outlook to understand the effects of value creation, against the nature of investments made. These insights may need data over a few months to a few years, even. For instance, marketing strategies may not bear fruit within a few days or weeks of initiation. It takes a long, sustained effort to realize value from marketing. The same can be said of infrastructure investments in software. In the short term, they may seem like high costs with low returns, but in the longer run, they will reap massive benefits. The urgency with which we need to launch and assess product adoption/feedback versus the time needed to evaluate the success of product strategy, to pivot or to persevere has to be balanced. Actions must be hastened, but decisions must be thought through.

There are, therefore, two types of insights we're considering in terms of product performance. The first tells us if our actions are working—is our product working well for the customer? The second tells us if our strategies are working—is our product working well for the business?

Is our product working well for the customer?

We identified features based on business investments/goals. We assigned value scores, identified costs, and found the smartest thing to build within the given constraints of the business. We then defined time-bound success metrics to help us to evaluate whether our feature is working well. We also put in effective mechanisms to capture quantitative and qualitative feedback from the consumers.

The metrics and feedback can give us a good hold on how close or far we are from meeting our success goals. However, as we build different features and work under the constraint of time and resources, we tend to make trade-offs. We also build product experience through multiple features, both in the product and also as part of the extended service around the product with support from the business functions.

The success metrics here are time-bound. They are also mostly time-bound to the near future (maybe three to five months), but measured over hours, days, or weeks, depending on the nature of the business. The typical metrics that we can capture at a feature level, that can point us towards the core goals of growth, influence, and sustainability are as follows:

- Number of new customers acquired
- Number of paying customers
- Retention rate
- Number of new leads
- Ratio of leads to conversions
- Number of renewals (subscribers)
- Engagement rates
- Number (and nature) of support requests received
- Time to convert (from lead to paying customer)
- Average time taken to complete flow
- Feature usage patterns (frequency of use, how many users use a feature, and so on)
- Feature adoption (drop off rates, completion of flow, workflow/ activity metrics, and so on)

These are only some indicators of performance. These indicators are also dependent on the nature of the product. B2C metrics could be different from B2B metrics. Moreover, the way we benchmark these metrics also matters.

Benchmarking

We already touched upon the idea of defining realistic and achievable metrics in the context of available business resources, time and other constraints, and product maturity, as well as our own ambitious goals. In this context, benchmarking against industry averages may not really be advisable, especially for an early stage of a product. This is partly because industry average benchmarks are not easily available. More so, if you are building a product that is disrupting an industry, the chances are that there are no benchmarks. Even as a competitive player in an industry with widespread demand, there may not exist benchmarks that are easily available.

It is possible to get caught in the trap of going after numbers that someone outside of our business defines for us. This can be quite damaging. We will be unable to reconcile our motivations and constraints with those of someone external to the business. Each business context is unique and setting goals that are pertinent to the sustenance and growth of the business, based on its unique context, is necessary.

In this context, vanity metrics must be pointed out. It is rather convenient to go after likes, views, and shares on social media. It can make us feel absolutely great about ourselves without adding a single ounce of value to the business. Sometimes, time is spent creating posts on social media, and feeling great about likes and views, when our customers are corporate decision-makers who aren't really looking for business partners on Facebook. Getting views on posts almost justifies the effort put into creating the posts, but this clearly misses the point.

Let's take hypothetical data for two products. Both the products measure the same metrics every quarter:

Product 1

Features	number of new customers acquired	number of paying customers	number of leads	number of customers lost
Features 1 and 2	50	0	200	0

Product 2

Features	number of new customers acquired	number of paying customers	number of leads	number of customers lost
Feature A	180	0	200	0

This data tells us a few notable things. One thing that stands out when comparing the two products is that the ratio between leads and new customers acquired is higher for product 2, than for product 1. More fundamentally, there seems to be no basis for comparing the metrics of these two products, even if we assume they belong to the same domain. What can be gleaned individually is that features 1 and 2 haven't contributed toward getting paying customers. This also hasn't led to any customer loss and similarly for feature A of product 2.

Metrics that validate or falsify success criteria

Comparing success metrics for a different business or product, or even considering industry benchmarks without context isn't going to help us to validate the success of our product. The only way to figure out whether any of this data is relevant is to see how it ties into any of the success criteria that we have.

Product 1

Features	number of new customers acquired	number of paying customers	number of leads	number of customers lost
Target success metric for features 1 and 2	100	70	120	NA
Actual data for features 1 and 2	50	0	200	0

Product 2

Features	number of new customers acquired	number of paying customers	number of leads	number of customers lost
Target success metrics for feature A	200	50	200	0
Actual data for feature A	180	0	200	0

Table: Target success metrics versus actuals; this is only an indicative simplified example

Now, if we compare these results against the defined success criteria for each feature, it gives us a much clearer indication of how far or close we are from the original goals. For product 1, features 1 and 2 were meant to bring in 100 new customers. They brought in 50, which is only 50% of the goal met. The paying customers metric was not met at all, but the number of leads was well above the mark. Customer retention or loss wasn't relevant at all. This is a good indicator that the product needs improvement in the approach to customer acquisitions and converting them to paying customers. Similarly, for product 2, there is some lag in acquiring new customers, but it is the conversion to paying customers that is clearly lagging.

Contextual qualitative insights

There may be multiple other minor and major indicators of success, and a relative comparison based on original goals versus those achieved will tell us where our product needs improvement. Sometimes, we may need to wait a week more for some potential leads in the pipeline that could convert into customers. Factors preventing success could include possible budget cycles in the customers' businesses that could be impacting their actual conversion to paying customers. Alternatively, there could be a change needed in the layout of the webpage or the placement of the purchase option. These aspects can be gleaned by digging deeper into what these numbers mean and their context.

However, these are still only the quantitative aspects. Contextual insights, user experience, adoption, usage frequencies, and so on can be complemented with qualitative data. Interesting questions when seeking qualitative information about the product experience could be as follows:

- What was the most frustrating problem we solved for a customer?
- What was the highest expression of appreciation we received from a customer?
- What was the worst complaint we received from a customer?
- Which customer persona is missing from our product users?
- When was the last time a customer who dropped off, came back and revived their activity?
- Which cohort/user will most likely recommend our product to or influence other customers?

These questions can kindle a variety of contextual information gathering. Again, these are only indicative questions to start exploring aspects of the customer experience that we may find hard to quantify. The individual consumer context can offer a personal touch and make the data seem more relevant. It also helps us focus on the consumer without getting bogged down by just data.

At a feature level, these metrics offer great visibility into areas that need improvement or those that are already working in our favor. Where these metrics fall short is in telling us real insights about whether our product strategy is working well or not. They also do not tell us whether the decisions and trade-offs we made today will hurt us or help us in the long run. Many of the technical success criteria have a longer cycle of value realization. In the short term, making compromises on some product aspects (technical or functional) may work well. This will help us meet immediate timelines, beat competitors, and gain market share, but in the longer run this approach may drag us down.

It is these longer running strategic insights that will help us to take pivot or persevere decisions. In the preceding example, Feature 1 seems to failing to get paid customers. But that alone is not a compelling reason to pivot on our product strategy. It is very hard to objectively conclude this. Even if feature 1 is the crux of the product and epitomizes the riskiest proposition that our product is putting forward, the business must still dig deeper to find out what gap in the product experience was not anticipated, which we can discover from product usage or actual customer feedback. The Febreze case study in *Chapter 7, Track, Measure, and Review Customer Feedback,* tells us exactly this. We cannot possibly predict to the tee how the market will react to our product. However, we cannot pivot at the first sight of trouble. Pivoting is a decision that is based on how much investment the business can make on validating the riskiest proposition before resources run out. Alignment to strategy, therefore, needs a longer-term outlook. That brings us to the second part of the product insights.

Is our product working well for the business?

Businesses make investments on different areas of functions. When a product is core to the success of a business (either complementing the core business drivers or being a core driver itself), the investments that the business makes toward the product will determine how we channelize our resources toward creating value.

The Investment Game that we played as part of our product strategy is crucial to not only determining what to build but also to highlighting the most valuable goals for the business and also in determining whether the business is even investing in the right product goals.

We often miss out on this aspect of product insight. Sometimes, this is because product technology teams get treated as external to business strategy. However, having established that the goal setting and defining the Impact Driven Product is a collaborative, collectively owned activity, we can assume that business stakeholders will work closely with the product teams to define product direction and strategy.

The purpose of restricting the Investment Game to a limited amount of money is to enforce artificial constraints (of actual money available, human capital, partners, and so on) and to determine where the business wants to bet their biggest success on. So far, we have run this with a specific time frame in mind. We seek to answer, which aspects of the business do we want to channelize our resources to in the next 3 months in order to realize the most desired business outcomes?

However, in 3 months we may have insights about whether our product features (what and how) are working well. We might be asking if we made the right investments or went after the right goals (the why). The answers to this will tell us how well our product strategy is working. In order to do this, we will need to review the investments and outcomes over a longer period of time. For this, once again, let's look at the example of product 2 shown earlier in this chapter. Again, this is a hypothetical example of product performance for a select few metrics, but over four quarters.

Q1 investments made – product 2

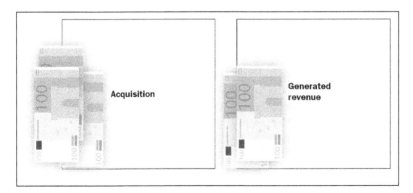

Q2 insights for product 2

Features	number of new customers acquired	number of paying customers
Goals	200	50
Feature A	180	0

Seeing that our acquisition strategy is working well, but that we are unable to generate revenue, let's say that the product investments for the next quarter will be made as shown in the following diagram:

Q2 investments made – product 2

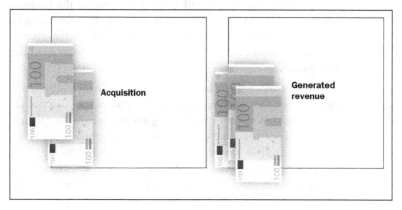

Q3 performance

Features	# new customers acquired	# paying customers
Goals	250	70
Feature B	240	20

Increasing the investments made to generate revenue seems to show minimal results. There is some progress, but not something that can justify the amount of investment made here. We could now analyze what we need to change about our product experience to convert more registered customers to paying users. So, let's say that we figure out that customer engagement may be an area of investment. Here are the product investments for Q3:

Q3 investments made – product 2

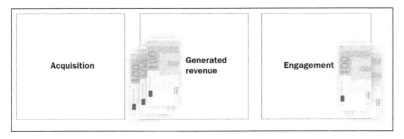

Q4 performance

Features	number of new customers acquired	number of paying customers
Goals	300	100
Feature C,D,E	280	50

Looking at the investments made on engagement and revenue generation, with the goal of increasing the number of paying customers, this strategy seems to be somewhat working. Let's say now that we continue to invest in these three areas of the product for the next quarter:

Q4 investments made – product 2

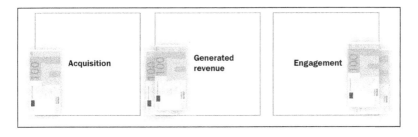

Q5 performance

Features	number of new customers acquired	number of paying customers
Goals	350	150
Feature F	250	60

Individually, each product strategy seems to be working well when looking at investments made in each quarter, as we can see in the following figure:

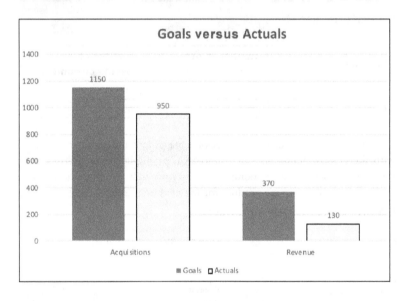

The following is a split of how product investments were made across the four quarters:

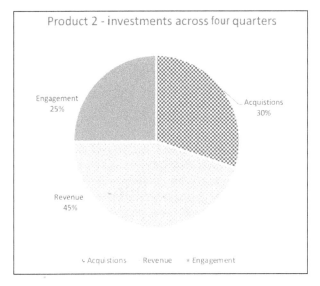

The correlation between investments made, product goals, and actual realization may be represented as shown in the following figures:

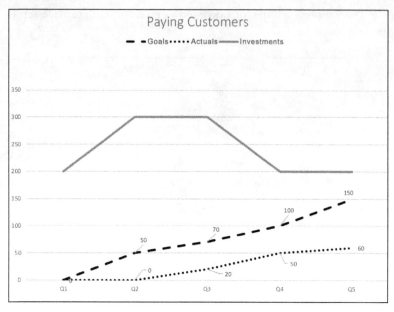

It appears that where investments have been made in acquisitions, the product has delivered fairly well. However, the product has failed to deliver revenue in terms of paying customers. Even though the business has made 45% of its product investment toward gaining paying customers, and then some more in terms of engagement, which was also intended to meet the revenue metrics, the product strategy here hasn't really kicked off here. This could mean two things: one, the investment made is not enough to create significant value in the product, or two, the product features aren't making the best use of the investment made here. Understanding this will mean getting into the details of product-level success metrics and learning more from the available pool of new customers, which is growing, but they are not ready to pay.

Another aspect that we can see here is where the business is failing to invest. Individual feature metrics may be targeted at finding out how we meet the feature goals. What about the overall business metrics? For instance, do we know if we are losing customers along the way? Do we know the channel through which we are acquiring customers? What do we lose if we don't increase our marketing and reach beyond the current channels? Will our acquisition strategy still continue to work for us?

We seem to be slowly increasing the number of paying customers, but seem to fall too short on meeting the goals. Are our goals for paying customers far too high? What about other factors such as actual revenue numbers? Are a smaller number of users bringing in higher value? How do product investments compare against similar investments made in other aspects of the business? How do we compare the actual investments made versus profits? Should we take a hit on acquiring new customers, while we change our strategy for revenue? Should we discover new channels for growth? Is it time to pivot? The answers to some of these questions may be far more relevant when seen as a trend across time, rather than looking at them in the context of quarter-to-quarter performance.

Delayed gratification

Especially in areas such as marketing and reach, the cycle time is much longer for us to even see the results of our investments working. In order to get the right kind of leads, we may need to experiment with different channels, content, messaging, and product experiences. We will still not reap immediate results. The trend could look something like this: a high investment is made initially on marketing and reach, and it doesn't show desired results until Q4, where the continued investments made start to show results:

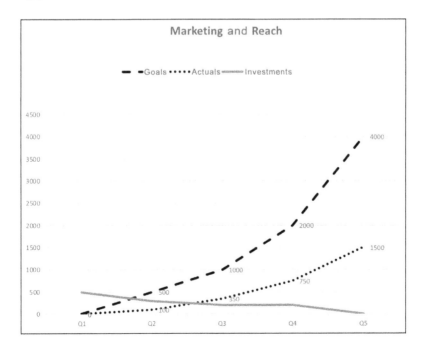

The same can be said for application stability, security, privacy, or any of the technical success metrics. Sometimes, the success of these investments is the absence of a harmful incident that threatens the product or the business. For some products dealing with highly confidential information, even a single incident of security breach can cause a lot of damage. Anticipating this and planning for the long term will require a different mindset and different data trends and insights.

Focusing on the short-term metrics can give the product much-needed acceleration to meet the needs of the customer and to react to the demands from the market. However, looking at longer-term trends and metrics can enable the business to invest in the right business aspects and look out for the longer-term benefits. This will lead to informed trade-offs, rather than looking only at the immediate performance of the product.

Looking at micro-level, short-term indicators alone cannot tell us how to steer our product in the ambiguous business ecosystem. For instance, if we are the first movers and are growing slowly and steadily, delivering on adoption and revenue per our success metrics, should we continue to run with the same pace or scale? If we were to scale, what opportunities or threats exist? If a new competitor emerges, making huge investments in marketing a similar product and capturing market share, we may have to factor that in our investments. This could also enable us to make informed decisions on which aspects of the product to invest in or to not enhance, in view of the macro-level factors of market opportunities and the threat from competition.

Summary

In this chapter, we discovered that qualitative and quantitative metrics are both necessary to getting a balanced view about product performance. Short-term metrics can help us to navigate through bottlenecks in product adoption, user experience, and so on and help us to respond better to the external market dynamics. However, relying purely on short-term metrics won't help us to think through product strategy for the longer term. Planning for the long term will require making investments now, which will not yield us immediate results. It also requires understanding how the product strategy aligns to the business drivers and the larger opportunities and threats from the market that are not necessarily visible in the short term.

The first part of the book was about deciding what to build in our Impact Driven Product. The second part, of which this is the concluding chapter, was about determining if we are building the right product by reviewing our scope, incorporating product feedback into our product and reviewing our progress based on metrics and investments made in Key Business Outcomes. The next few chapters, in the third part of the book, will help us evaluate our processes and assess if we are building our product right.

—Part Three—

Are we building the product right?

9

ELIMINATE
WASTE – DON'T
ESTIMATE!

Estimations are an integral part of software development. They are required for understanding the costs and effort involved in development, to analyze the impact of scope on time and budgets. When we try to arrive at accurate delivery timelines, we tend to attach a lot of importance to estimates. We try to get very specific and accurate with our estimates. However, an accurate estimate sounds like an oxymoron. Product teams surely need a way to understand costs, complexity, risks, resources, people with specific skills, and so on in order to be able to plan the smartest way to deliver the Impact Driven Product. It's not just about meeting timelines and staying within budgets. Are product teams wasting their effort and time by focusing on the wrong details (such as accurate estimates)? Are we compromising on individuals and interactions by focusing on tools and processes? How do we keep our focus on outcomes and eliminate wasteful processes that focus on outputs?

We will address the following questions in this chapter:

- Why do we need estimates?
- Why can estimates not be accurate?
- What should be the outcome of an estimation discussion?

Why do we need estimates?

If I were to ask you how long it would take you to reach Bengaluru from Chennai, India, would you be able to answer accurately? Probably not. Your lack of familiarity with the two places and how far apart they are, combined with the lack of specifics about what mode of transport, weather conditions, and so on, will render it difficult for you to accurately answer. However, we can answer this question better by building up a familiarity with the domain (the two cities and how far apart they are) and the implementation (what type of vehicle, under what weather conditions, and so on).

A smart alternative would be to look up Google Maps and find a roughly indicative answer to my question, without getting familiar with the domain, but with some assumptions on implementation. However, in whichever way we answer that question, we still don't know why the travel is needed or who is travelling? What does reaching the destination signify for this person? What if the traveler cannot make it to the destination? So, we not only need to know the domain and implementation details, we also need to understand the user context, goals, and risks involved.

What if I told you that I need to get to Bengaluru from Chennai by tonight because I have an important business meeting to attend? What if a heart surgeon has to reach Bengaluru from Chennai to see a critical care patient? What if a college student is making plans to attend his favorite rock star's concert in Bengaluru? The answers to these questions are not best fulfilled by an effort estimate. Instead, it is about exploring the best possible ways for each of those people to reach their destination. The user context in terms of their motivations, emotional state, urgency of their needs, and so in, is very important. What is also important is how much they are willing to spend to find a solution to their problem and what other alternatives they are considering.

Estimates can be provided if we know the domain and implementation specifics, but a meaningful implementation plan cannot be arrived at when we don't understand business outcomes, customer goals, risks, and market realities. We need to ask ourselves if we would want to stick to output-level details (estimates) or outcome-level details (an implementation plan). Our success is in how well we execute the travel plan, not in how accurately we predicted the time. Accurate estimates may make us reliable and accountable for productivity, but a well-laid out implementation plan makes us more reliable and accountable for outcomes. The strength of a product team is not in whether we stick to a committed date, but whether we can commit to a business outcome.

Product teams therefore must answer the following questions, which are not answered by the engineering team in isolation, but by the product teams as a group:

- What are the possible ways that we can meet the success criteria?
- What's the smartest way to test our riskiest proposition?
- Should we build or buy?
- Do we have the skills and resources to make this possible?
- What can I not afford to delay and should build today?
- What are we dependent on to ensure our success?
- What is the effort and complexity involved?
- What are our risks and what trade-offs are we making?

All these questions must be answered in the context defined by the following factors:

- Key Business Outcomes
- Customer value proposition
- Success metrics
- Internal and external constraints

Why can estimates not be accurate?

Estimating software development effort is not just a well-established routine anymore. I'm afraid that it is evolving into a branch of science! For decades now, software teams have tried to come up with various methods to predict timelines.

About 15 years ago, I used Function Points as a way to assess the size of an application, based on how much input / output data the application had to handle. This was at a stage where a system view of a software was more prevalent and the applications were mostly about data flow. There was little user input. User experience was never discussed. This meant that software developers could be given requirement specifications, with details of what field to input and what to validate for each input. Here, implementation specifics were closely tied to the requirements specifications. A change in implementation specifics or the addition of a new field to capture, would impact the size of the application in terms of Function Points. Managing scope was the most important task at hand. We sized scope, not effort.

The next variation was Use Case Points. This was sort of a bridge between the system's view and a user's view of an application. This tracked all the use cases of a system, but the sizing was similar to Function Points. We considered user transactions, along with some weightage for technical complexity and so on, but these were still waterfall methods with bulky requirement specifications that instructed developers on exactly what to build. I have written requirement documents with **UML (Unified Modeling Language)** diagrams that showed use cases, classes, state charts, and system touchpoints. Once again, this was less about coding effort and more about project sizing. Scope negotiation again was critical. Scope had to be finalized and signed off before handing over to development. Any changes thereafter would go through an elaborate change request approval process.

The problem with Function Points and Use Case Points was that they were dependent on knowing all the details of implementation beforehand. Budgets and timelines were based on the application size, which in turn was determined by a system that locked in an implementation plan even before we began development. This meant that any new discovery during development would have to go through an elaborate change management process, resulting in rework, loss of time, and too many approval processes, since it involved a change in timeline/budgets.

The Agile manifesto was created as a way to counter some of these drawbacks. The Agile manifesto called for responding to change, rather than following a plan. This was such a refreshing change from the way projects were previously run. There were no bulky requirement documents. There was no upfront freeze on implementation specifics. This gave more power to the software developers, since implementation could now evolve to meet needs and respond to feedback. Still, businesses needed to understand the cost of building and subsequent changes. Someone had to tell a business how much this would cost and how long it would take, because budgets were limited or had to be decided early on. If we build incrementally, how can we establish scope size upfront? So, effort estimations and managing scope became critical.

It is easy to argue the case for estimating in days. Why can't we simply state how many days/weeks it would take to build a given scope? However, what does a day mean? Is it eight hours of uninterrupted work or is it more like six and a half hours, given that I have to attend meetings, respond to emails and eat? Developers had to agree whether to estimate in man-days or ideal days. They had to remember this decision every time they estimated (which was pretty much every week or two weeks). Each time someone new joined the team, they had to bring them on board with this agreement. This could slow down the team, instead of increasing productivity.

There were also other open questions here: what if a task took only three hours to complete? What if something else took 10 days to complete? Will it take a less experienced developer the same time to code this as someone more experienced/skilled?

Estimating effort for smaller scope with higher details on domain and user context, could be more accurate. So, user stories became necessary. User stories follow the INVEST principles. They are meant to be Independent, Negotiable, Valuable, Estimable, Small, and Testable. Still, estimating effort in days was not accurate because of all the preceding open questions. So, we had to somehow break from an absolute effort to relative sizing. If we could agree that user story1 was the size of a grape (it was as small, easy to eat), then we could try to figure out whether user story2 was also a grape or an orange (requiring more effort to eat, bigger) or a watermelon (much bigger and more complex to eat):

User story	Fruit size
User story 1	Grape
User story 2	Orange
User story 3	Orange
User story 4	Watermelon
User story 5	Orange
User story 6	Grape
User story 7	Grape

We could then use these sizes to establish how many grapes, oranges, and watermelons a team was able to eat in an iteration:

Iteration	# of grapes	# of oranges	# of watermelons
Week 1	1	1	
Week 2			1
Week 3	2		
Week 4		1	

Now, if we assign a number to a grape, orange, or watermelon, it becomes a story point. For instance, we could say that a grape is 1, an orange is 2 (twice as big and complex as a grape), and a watermelon is 5 (more than twice as big and complex as an orange). We can replace the preceding table with story points and count the number of points:

Iteration	# of fruits	Story points
Week 1	1 grape + 1 orange	3
Week 2	1 watermelon	5
Week 3	2 grapes	2
Week 4	1 orange	2

This gives us team velocity (how many fruits we can eat in a given time or how many story points we can complete in an iteration). We could then compare this over time, and this would tell us our burn rate. How many fruits do we eat on an average every week?

Now this seems like a great way to get away from thinking about actual days or hours, and instead focus on the size, complexity, risks, resources needed, and so on. For instance, cutting a watermelon would need knives. The ideal way to create user stories would be to try and make them all as small as possible. If they were all grapes, it would just become so much easier. We could count all the grapes, and we could assess our capacity to eat grapes, and then we could forecast how many grapes we could eat in the next six months. So, it appears that if we come up with the right user stories, we can get pretty good at estimating accurately. However, it isn't as easy as it sounds.

There are many aspects that can influence our plans (based on estimates). Here are few such aspects:

- **Team composition can change**: The people who estimated stories as oranges may move out of the team to be replaced with new people. New people could bring in other perspectives and ideas. What the original team thought was an orange could turn out to be a grape because there are now better ideas and easier ways to eat.
- **Technology and business context assumptions change**: Technology changes can make it easier or harder to build something. We may have estimated a user feature as 10 watermelons and 5 oranges, assuming that we had to build it from scratch, but our product could have matured to a state where we could integrate with an existing software rather than build one. The feature could now be 3 oranges.

- **Familiarity increases**: A steady team of developers working on the same product for a long period of time will gain a much higher level of familiarity. They may get influenced by their knowledge of the current way of doing things and may be able to find a faster way to implement. An orange can be eaten as easily as a grape.

- **Biases can kick-in**: No matter how much we try to position story sizing as an effort sizing activity and not a time estimation. I have seen that people naturally sink into thinking about efforts in days and hours. Also, having an expert on the team can make people submissive and consequently, conformation bias can kick in. Of course, asking people to call out their estimates in the blind (such as Planning Poker, which is an estimation technique that can help teams arrive at consensus-based estimates) can help in this, but eventually team culture will determine whether the expert will force down their ideas on the team. They will say, "I know how to do this. So, it is an orange if I say that it is an orange."

- **Decision fatigue sets in**: Typical estimation sessions are conducted for a backlog of user stories. At the beginning, everyone comes in with a fresh mind and discussions are detailed. As time passes, and the team has to make many decisions, there is a tendency to rush through the stories, without discussing details. Estimates are thrown for the sake of getting the meeting over with. A team member might say, "Some of us think that it's an orange. Some of us think that it's a grape. Ah, I'm too tired. Let's go with grape."

If the purpose of story point-based estimates is to forecast future velocity (how much scope can we deliver in a given amount of time), then all the preceding aspects actually hinder us from doing this. There are too many variables that affect our forecasting. A side-effect of tracking velocity is also that the focus shifts from outcomes (did we deliver something of value?) to output (was the team productive? Did we eat as many fruits as we said we would?). We forget that eating grapes and oranges is not the goal.

Budget allocation strategies may have to change if we do away with estimates. In an evolving product, for a business operating under ambiguous market conditions, budget planning needs to be iterative too. While we still need to know the *cost* of a feature idea, accurate effort estimates cannot be our only way to arrive at that cost.

What should be the outcome of an estimation discussion?

Estimation discussions, in my experience, have one very valuable outcome. It's not the story points, but it's the conversations and interactions that happen around the story details. As the team builds familiarity with the user context, business goals, existing framework, technology options, assumptions, and so on, there are valuable ideas that take shape.

Breaking down a user story into tasks (or things to do) helps the team align on the best implementation approach. The pros and cons of an approach are discussed. The trade-offs (what we will not get by following this plan) are discussed. Assumptions are challenged. Risks are identified. Ideation kicks in. The most important outcomes from an estimation session are these ideas, tasks, and questions.

So, if we flip this around, and conduct implementation discussions instead of estimation sessions, then we can expect that estimates will be just one minor detail to derive. We saw in *Chapter 5, Identify the Impact Driven Product*, that each feature idea can be rated on a scale of 0-10, based on the cost to build that feature idea. The rating was based not just on estimates but also based on the complexity, technology readiness, risks, dependencies, available skill sets (technical and supporting business functions), and resources (hardware and software).

In order for us to arrive at this cost rating, we can follow this process:

1. **Break down a feature idea into success metrics**: As discussed in *Chapter 5, Identify the Impact Driven Product*, we can identify the SMART success metrics, owners, and timelines to measure success.

2. **Identify success metrics that need technical implementation**: The cost for activities that can best be handled manually (for instance, content creation in the case of ArtGalore art catalog newsletter), can be evaluated differently. Other business functions can evaluate their implementation costs for success metrics of they own. We can decide when a feature is done (can fully deliver impact) based on which success criteria must be fulfilled in the product for us to launch it. In the case of time-bound feature ideas (where we are required to launch within a certain date / time period due to market compulsions, such as in the case of ArtGalore), we can identify which success criteria can deliver the most impact and arrive at a doable / not doable decision, as described here in step 6.

3. **Add details for every success metric**: The intent of the details is to increase familiarity with the user context, business outcomes, and internal/external constraints.

4. **Facilitate an implementation discussion for one feature idea, across all its success metrics**: The smaller the number of items to discuss, the fewer the chances of decision fatigue. Enable teams to ideate on implementation, and arrive at tasks to do, risks, dependencies, open questions, assumptions, and so on.

5. **Call out assumptions**: Team size, definition of done (are we estimating for development complete or testing complete or production ready) and so on, also need to be agreed upon.

6. **In the case of time-bound feature ideas**: Arrive at a doable / not doable decision. Can we meet the timeline with the current scope/implementation plan? If not, can we reduce the scope or change the implementation plan? What support do we need to meet the timeline? The intent should be to answer *how* to meet a success criterion. The intent is not to answer *when* we will be able to deliver. Team velocity itself becomes irrelevant, since it is no longer about maintaining a predictable pace of delivery, but it is now about being accountable for delivering impact.

   Capture these details from the discussion. This is based on how we identify a cost rating for the feature idea based on these discussions.

On a scale of 0-10, a feature idea effectively falls into two categories: the 0-5 low-cost bucket (*doable*) which would give us *quick wins* and *nice to haves* and the 5-10 high-cost bucket (*not doable*), which would give us the *strategic wins* and *deprioritize* buckets. So, while we evaluate the implementation details, the question we're trying to answer is: what box in the impact-cost matrix does this feature idea fall in?

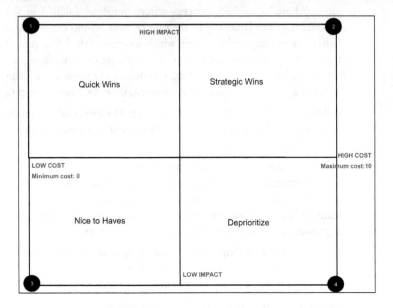

So, we can do the same for each success metric under a feature idea, as shown in the following image. A feature idea could have many success metrics, some of which could be *quick wins* some of which could be *strategic wins*. Some could be *nice to haves* and some are in *deprioritize* (depending on the impact score of the feature idea):

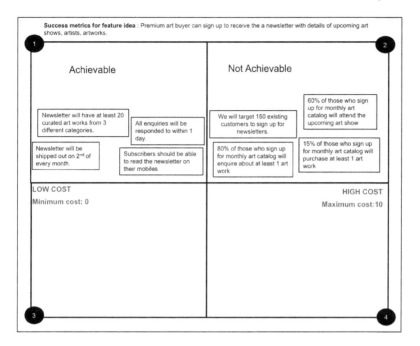

Success metrics for feature idea : Premium art buyer can sign up to receive the a newsletter with details of upcoming art shows, artists, artworks.

We can then evaluate if the feature idea can still deliver value with the quick wins and strategic wins success metrics. We can assess dependencies and so on and then arrive at the overall cost rating for the feature idea. We can arrive at a doable / not doable (within given constraints) decision with a much higher level of confidence.

This allows us to set time-bound goals for developers to work on. The measure of success for product teams becomes the outcomes they have been instrumental in delivering, not the number of story points they have delivered. This can help us to structure teams based on the shorter-term quick-win work streams and longer-term strategic work streams. It also takes away the need to track velocity, and we can now focus on outcomes and success metrics.

Summary

In this chapter, we learned that effort estimation, or story sizing is useful as part of the implementation plan. However, in cases where our implementation is to proceed with a buy or partner approach (instead of a build), we don't need to estimate effort at all. Although we still need to get to the details about the cost of the implementation plan, based on the complexity, technology readiness, risks, dependencies, available skill sets (technical and supporting business functions), and resources (hardware and software). The intent of our implementation discussions should be about finding the smartest way to implement a feature idea. Estimating the effort should be one minor aspect of product implementation.

Teams should be ready to embrace effort estimations when needed and discard the need for estimations based on context and needs, rather than following a plan/process for the sake of following it. The emphasis should be on the interactions that happen when arriving at an implementation plan. Isn't this the essence of the "individuals and interactions over processes and tools," as stated in the Agile manifesto?

We have now figured out one aspect of our product building process and ensured that we are not bound by our internal processes and productivity metrics. Instead, we are motivated by internal and external constraints and bound by the outcomes, so that we can deliver an Impact Driven Product. While deciding the smartest way to deliver impact, product teams also need to understand what they must build versus what they can buy. Let's explore this aspect in the next chapter.

~ 10 ~

ELIMINATE WASTE – DON'T BUILD WHAT WE CAN BUY

When arriving at a doable / not doable decision for a feature idea, product teams must not shy away for considering whether there is a need to build something at all. If there is an opportunity for teams to buy an existing solution or engage in a partnership with someone who offers a service/ solution, we need to be open to considering that.

This decision of build versus buy versus partner versus nothing at all depends to a large extent upon how well our solution meets the needs of the customer and what our cost-impact comparison looks like.

This chapter addresses the following topics:

*   Building what the customer values the most
*   Feature black holes that eat up a team's time
*   Parameters to consider to enable a build versus buy decision

Selling an idea

"Perfection is achieved, not when there is nothing more to add, but when there is nothing left to take away."

- Antoine de Saint-Exupéry

Sir Richard Branson once had to travel to the British Virgin Islands. The airline cancelled his flight because there weren't enough passengers. So, he hired a plane and wrote up on a blackboard the price of a one-way ticket to the British Virgin Islands. He went around selling tickets to the stranded passengers. This is how his airline business was launched.

Of course, it took much more investment, creativity, and business acumen to make a fully fledged airline business. However, selling tickets for the flight was the essential first step. To sell tickets, Sir Richard Branson didn't need to build his own plane. He didn't need elaborate props. A hired plane and a blackboard was enough. This was only because the sales proposition and the market need were compelling.

If we don't have a compelling solution to a market need, then it probably doesn't matter how well made our product is. Product building, therefore, needs to be as close as possible to market needs. We need to have a finger on the pulse of the market. We will explore more on this aspect in *Chapter 11, Eliminate Waste – Data Versus Opinions*. The metrics at this stage should drive what needs to be in the product.

Sales is one of the best ways to get a sense of what the customer is willing to pay for. It is a great way to arrive at our testable hypotheses. They tells us what is the most valuable part of the product that a customer is willing to pay for. Customer support, on the other hand, is our lens into adoption metrics. This tells us what the worst product experience is that a customer is willing to tolerate and still stay with us.

There is a reason strong enough for product teams (especially product managers) to get their hands dirty. They must sell and support the product. This does not mean that they accompany a sales person on a customer visit or look at customer support request queues. This calls for coming up with the sales pitch and driving a sales conversation with a potential customer. It also means supporting a customer when they raise issues with the product. It is this reality check that will ensure that the product teams keep their feet firmly on the ground.

Coming up with a sales pitch will help us find out what is the most compelling need of our customers. It will help us to identify which aspect of our product appeals to our customers and how our product excites or underwhelms them. It will help us to refine the value proposition to the very basics. Taking a founder's word, or a sales person's word, about what a customer wants isn't enough. We must get out of the building and find the answer for ourselves.

We also need to steel our hearts against finding out that our product isn't what our customers are willing to pay for. This insight is best derived when we haven't built much, so that a rework doesn't cost us or kill our business. Getting customer feedback early is the best part of selling. It is possible to sell without having a product. To sell, you just need a compelling solution to a pressing need. For eons now, religion had sold to us an idea that we can have a better afterlife if we pray and donate to religious causes. The afterlife isn't a product that exists. It exists only in our imagination (collective imagination, actually). Yet, so many people pray religiously and donate without question. Indeed, some amazing marketing and great influencers ensure that the idea of an afterlife is well propagated. It addresses a core emotional need for so many people; so much that they're willing to invest their time and money into a concept that has no evidence. Religion presents a compelling solution to what seems like a pressing need: we want to feel secure about what happens after death. After all, praying is a small investment to make in return for a great afterlife.

Without espousing, censuring, or condoning the strategy of religion, let's agree that selling an idea has been around for long enough now. Many months before my start-up was even set up, we had the chance to interact with many conference organizers, speakers, event sponsors, and regular conference attendees. We spent considerable time talking to every person in the events and conferences ecosystem. We tried to find out what problems they faced. What did they desire from a conference? How well did our product idea address their needs? We were able to glean patterns from the data that we had gathered by speaking to so many folks. Then, we spent a few days brainstorming about our end-to-end service design. We tried to figure out how our idea of a mobile app, that would serve as a digital agenda and networking and sponsorship medium, would fit into the ecosystem. The deciding factor for us was to figure out who was going to pay us for meeting their needs. Conference organizers and event sponsors were our biggest bets.

However, we had to test our hypothesis. So, instead of building a mobile app, we created a slick slide deck with wonderfully designed screens that highlighted the key features in the app. I'd like you to refer back to the discussion in *Chapter 6*, *Managing the Scope of an Impact Driven Product*, about identifying the impactful product for a market where technology viability exists. In our case, the viability of building a mobile app already existed. What we had to test was whether event organizers would pay for such a solution, and, if so, how much they would be willing to pay; also, whether this amount would be enough to be a compelling proposition for us to pursue, to build a product at all. Our presentation deck had only well-designed screens of features, which we felt would get the conference organizers excited. We tried a combination of features and had different versions of the deck. We also came up with a baseline amount, which we thought the organizers would be willing to pay for such a product.

Armed with nothing but a flashy slide deck and glib talk, we set up meetings with potential customers. This deck and glib talk won us two customers who were ready to pay more than the baseline amount we had in mind. We learned an important lesson that there was a lot we could validate about our product without even having a product.

When we think of a service or a product, we tend to obsess about the service or product itself by asking: how do we improvise it? How do we make it stand apart from competitors? How do we make it appealing? What is the most impactful product to build?

What got you here won't get you there

Every stage of building a business demands a different maturity from the product. So, it would be futile to assume that we could always sell with a well-made slide deck and no real product to support it. However, the mindset about trying to gauge the pulse of the market before building anything is what we need to inculcate. How smartly can we figure out what our customers will pay for? Also, how can we figure out if we stop offering something, and will our customers continue to pay us?

At every stage of product building, we need to attempt to find the answers to both these questions, but our strategy to find these answers must evolve continually. For a well-matured product with a large customer base, it may not be possible to find out these answers merely by speaking to a few select customers (*Chapter 11*, *Eliminate Waste – Data Versus Opinions*, discusses the futility of doing this). However, we can introduce product feature teasers that can be rolled out to a large customer base and gather data from this. Pricing plans can be used to test which features or feature plans draw more interest from our target group.

In my start-up, we had, in fact, experimented with pricing quite a bit. In the early stages of product development, we didn't show our pricing plans on the website. We instead sent out customized product brochures to anyone who enquired on our website. This gave us ample leeway to try different combinations of features and different pricing sets. We also found out that our customers responded better when our price was not a round number. For instance, people responded better to a product priced as Rs. 67,700 rather than Rs 65,000. As we started getting repeat customers and referrals through customers, we figured out which pricing worked best. In the initial stages, we were talking only to small businesses and were dealing directly with the decision-makers. So, the impression that our pricing and product created on that individual mattered. However, when we started talking to bigger enterprise clients, some of these tactics didn't work. They had isolated teams that make product buying decisions, and we couldn't afford to be random in our pricing. We had to freeze on the pricing and feature bundles. We couldn't afford to waste time and experiment with pricing anymore. This is when we started to put up our pricing on the website.

Of course, these findings may have been quirky and unique to our product and market situation. Yet, the possibility that we could experiment with such aspects of the product excited us. The same mindset needs to be carried into what goes into our product at every stage of product building. Just because we have a larger customer base, it doesn't mean that we need to build a feature because we think it's useful for customers or because we feel it's a cool thing to build. Even when it is a feature that you need, you must ask if you really should build it. So if you're asking, "What should we build?", I'm going to respond with a counter question: "What would you rather not build?"

To build or not to build

Most teams tend to get carried away when seeing a product backlog that has features that offer a great opportunity to employ cool, cutting edge tech. Everyone wants to get their hands on it. It excites the team to go and build a product, even when there are so many products available on the market that can meet business needs quite well.

There are two broad categories of a product in terms of the value that it can produce. The feature can be an enabler or it can be a differentiator. We briefly discussed enablers and differentiators in *Chapter 5, Identify the Impact Driven Product*. An enabler is something that can help to support the core business impact. The enabler by itself may not be core to the business, but it helps to deliver or measure business impact. A differentiator, in contrast, is the business itself. One or more core aspects of the business depend on the differentiator. This is what qualifies as the IP (intellectual property, which is the intangible value created from patents, copyright, or creativity) of a product. Without this differentiator (or secret sauce), your business has no edge over the competition. When a feature is easy to copy, then soon enough our competitors will follow suit. They will learn from our mistakes and gaps in product experience and offer better value to customers. After all, the second mouse gets the cheese.

Even enablers can give a competitive advantage to our business, purely by helping the business to respond or scale to market needs. For example, banks that undertake digital transformations are essentially looking at online banking solutions as enablers. Their core banking model hasn't changed, but they are looking at digital channels to enable their existing strength. Digital solutions help to improve customer experience and reach, while reducing the cost of operations. Mobile apps act as a channel for digital banking. They can give the first banks that adopt them, a competitive edge. The enabler acts as a differentiator for a while, but then, mobile apps are easy to replicate, and subsequent versions from competitors will improve upon user experience and customer impact.

In general, if our product feature is a differentiator, then it is best to build it in-house. This gives the business the maximum leverage of being able to shape up the product, giving us full control on what we offer and how we offer it. However, if our product feature is an enabler, then the first decision to make is whether there is an existing solution that we could leverage. The following are some of the aspects that we want to consider when evaluating an off-the-shelf solution:

- How well can it meet our needs?
- Can it deliver on all of our success criteria?
- Does it integrate well with the rest of our product?
- Does it meet our pricing needs?
- Does it have unreasonable maintenance overheads?
- Is it hard to on-board?

The chances are that if we look hard enough, there is usually a solution to be found. We need to ask these questions before we decide to build from scratch:

1. Is the feature a core differentiator for the business?

2. Are our functional flows processed as standard and can they be met by an off-the-shelf product?

3. Is it critical for this feature to be rolled out with our branding?

4. Do we have specific/unique legal, compliance, and regulatory requirements that cannot be fulfilled by an off-the-shelf product?

5. Does the commercial proposition work well for us?

6. Does it integrate well with the rest of the technology stack used in our core product?

7. Is it easy to purchase, set up, and get started with the off-the-shelf product?

8. Is there a model of support for the off-the-shelf product that can meet our needs?

9. Do we have a partner who can build this for us?

10. Do we have the time and people to provide the oversight needed in order ensure that we have the right product delivered?

Based on the answers to the preceding questions described, for a feature idea that is an enabler, we can generally interpret whether or not to build the feature from scratch:

Questions	Build	Buy
Is the feature a core differentiator for the business?	Yes	No
Are our functional flows processed as standard and can they be met by an off-the-shelf product?	No	Yes
Is it critical for this feature to be rolled out with our branding and the off-the-shelf product offers no customized branding?	Yes	No
Do we have specific/unique legal, compliance, regulatory requirements that cannot be fulfilled by an off-the-shelf product?	Yes	No
Does the commercial proposition work better if we buy instead of build?	No	Yes
Does it integrate well with the rest of the technology stack used in our core product?	No	Yes
Is it easy to purchase, setup and get started with the off-the-shelf product?	No	Yes
Is there a model of support for the off-the-shelf product that can meet our needs?	No	Yes

This can serve as a guideline for deciding where to invest a product team's time.

Feature black holes that suck up a product team's time

Even when product backlogs are groomed well, there is a type of donkey work or feature black hole that swallows up team time. This kind of grunt work slowly creeps in and before you know it, a significant amount of the team time gets sucked up into it. It could come in as requests from powerful folks in leadership. It could come as a result of frustration with operational tools. It even creeps in as spillovers from heavy processes. For instance, if every request for new hardware, infrastructure, stationery, and so on has to go through an elaborate approval process, then the amount of time the team spends just waiting on approvals to be processed can be a process waste. So, the teams may end up using suboptimal solutions to work around the approval rules.

Such feature black holes are nonenabler and nondifferentiator work, which serve only to assuage the structural and cultural needs of internal teams. For instance, when we're a co-located small team and when the product is in the early stages of development, we may start off by tracking customer support requests using simple sticky notes on a wall. The information and backlog are visible to everyone, and we can co-ordinate without the need of any digital tools.

However, when the product evolves, the customer base and the team expand, and the sticky notes on the wall won't suffice. We may need a digital solution that can handle incoming requests, prioritize them, assign requests to specific folks, and track them. We may easily find a popular tool in the market that can serve this need. When teams start building an internal solution to meet the customer support tracking needs, it becomes a feature black hole. There is no compelling reason for the team to build it other than their own prejudices or lack of awareness about existing solutions. Any amount of work spent on building such a feature is taking the team away from the goal of meeting Key Business Outcomes. Even when the Key Business Outcome of the business is about sustainability and reducing internal operational costs, we need to critically evaluate our impact scores, success metrics, and doable / not doable cost decisions to decide whether to build or buy.

Now, the limitation of a tool in the market (also a product) is that it works well for most cases across a broad spectrum of needs. So, expecting that an off-the-shelf tool will align to every quirky need of our business is neither reasonable nor practical. Naturally, there will be a learning curve or an adoption period, where we have to unlearn our existing ways of working and adapt to the ways of the new tool. I agree, in principle, that allowing a tool to dictate our ways of working doesn't sound very appealing.

On the other hand, building our own version of a support request tracking tool, that reaps us no business benefits, isn't the smartest usage of our time, is it? So, when should we invest time, mindshare, and resources into building anything? The answer is that only when what we build creates justifiable business impact or when it offers a value proposition to the customer that can differentiate our business or when no such product exists that will meet our needs should we consider building an enabler. We build something only if *not* building it would cause serious detriment to the product/business. This is a need that must be justified to invest in as a Key Business Outcome. To go back to our example, is the value proposition so compelling that the business wants to invest in building a customized ticketing system that meets our internal needs?

It is also natural that we may outgrow the potential of an off-the-shelf solution. Transitioning to another solution will come with its own cost. We may also discover that there exists no solution in the market that addresses our specific needs. Off-the-shelf products may not meet our pricing criteria or our scale. Such instances make a great case for evaluating whether this niche compelling internal needs or problems can give rise to a new line of products that we can create. Would this product even have a long-term impact and serve as a secondary channel of revenue? Can such a need become a differentiator for us?

If we arrive at such a compelling pitch, it makes absolute sense to pursue this. For instance, Amazon's AWS services today has a $10 trillion run rate and overshadows the e-commerce business of Amazon. Amazon Web Services (AWS) started as a by-product when trying to meet the specific scaling needs of Amazon's e-commerce business. The internal teams created a common set of infrastructure services to meet the scaling needs. These services laid the foundation of today's AWS. Amazon had a compelling solution to a problem that a lot of other companies were facing and they were all probably trying to build their own solutions to address their needs. Amazon saw the opportunity to make this a compelling business proposition too.

However, nonenabler and nondifferentiator work is also not to be confused with research or innovation. Exploring technology possibilities, building proofs of concepts, and finding innovative ways to deliver value, which cannot be addressed by off-the-shelf solutions (or even custom-built solutions), are the pure value that a technology team can offer to the product. They are essentially experiments into which a business is willing to invest. This is akin to the car makers devoting a lifetime to the innovations around internal combustion engines (as we saw in *Chapter 6, Manage the Scope of an Impact Driven Product*). We cannot put a timeline to research and development. Unlike building products that have a proven technology viability, research cannot be a time-bound activity, or have specifications for meeting Key Business Outcomes. It cannot be part of the core product building team's focus. On the other hand, for building an Impact Driven Product, it is of utmost importance to ensure that the product team channels all of its energies only toward what can maximize the impact.

Every product manager needs to keep asking these questions:

- How valuable is it for us to have this feature in our product?
- Is there a ready-made solution that can offer the same value? Should we then buy, rather than build?
- How damaging is it to *not* have this in our product?
- What would we rather build if not this? Is there something more valuable than this to which we should direct our time, mindshare, and resources?

The following flowchart is a quick reference for taking a build versus buy versus not to build:

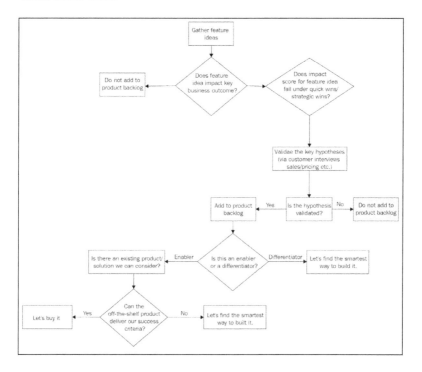

Summary

In this chapter, we learned that not every feature idea in the product needs to be built from scratch. Pruning the product backlog requires that we remove every item that doesn't add value to the business. A perfect backlog is one which has nothing left to take away.

Now that we have a product backlog that is lean and has only the very bare necessity features, we can streamline our teams based on the nature of outcomes that the feature can deliver and the response time needed to deliver on a feature. We will review how to streamline our processes in the next chapter.

11

ELIMINATE WASTE – DATA VERSUS OPINIONS

Once product development is underway, there are new feature ideas that will make their way into the product backlog. Having a data strategy can help us to evaluate new feature ideas and how our product performs in terms of success metrics. As we saw in *Chapter 7, Track, Measure, and Review Customer Feedback* we need to track, measure, and review customer feedback. We need to seek qualitative and quantitative insights. However, teams can be easily distracted when looking at the wrong data and biases. We need to eliminate wasteful processes in how we seek and interpret data. Product teams need to have a data strategy as an inherent part of their way of working.

Accordingly, this chapter will address the following topics:

- Defining the hypothesis that we seek to validate
- The problems with data

Defining the hypothesis

> *"If you don't know where you're going, any road will take you there."* -
> *Lewis Carroll*

Product feedback can come in many ways. *Chapter 7, Track, Measure, and Review Customer Feedback,* outlined some of the internal and external channels used to gather feedback. The problem is that when there is a lot of input from all these channels, we can get overwhelmed. There can be distraction from having too many voices in our ears. We don't know which voice to respond to because we often don't know where we're headed. Many times, businesses respond by listening to the loudest voice they can hear.

After all, the squeaky wheel gets the grease! A complaint on social media, or a suggestion from a close friend or a respected advisor, can suddenly become our focus of interest. It is indeed important that we respond to an influential consumer, whose opinion can cause damage to our brand. However, not every instance requires that we change our product because one user (however influential) complained. We can manage expectations with messaging, PR, and customer service too.

In fact, early-stage products frequently fall into this trap of getting feedback and advice, and not knowing which to heed and which to ignore. If you're a parent, you probably know what I mean. Raising an infant is one of the most challenging times for a parent. When we're fumbling about with no experience in having to handle a delicate infant, any support seems welcome. We look to our parents, neighbors, doctors, friends, and the internet to constantly check if we're doing the right thing. However, one untimely burp from the baby is all that is needed for advice to flood in. Grandparents, neighbors, and random strangers on the street advise you on what your baby is going through, how to hold him, what to feed him, or not feed him, and why you need to be a better parent. When we're in unsure territory and need all the help we can get, it's difficult to turn down advice. However, free advice soon becomes a bane. Knowing whose advice matters and more importantly knowing if we even need advice, is important. Every parent sooner or later figures this out and so should product teams!

Working around strongly opinionated stakeholders requires people management skills. Having a data strategy as an inherent way to make product decisions can help us to navigate the quagmire of opinions. Knowing how to leverage data to drive decisions and curb opinions is a key skill for product managers today. Data is key to learning about a product's success. Finding the pulse of the consumer is an important aspect of product building. We need to know whether we're headed in the right direction, whether our features are being used or not, who is using them, and how to measure the success of what we're building. On the other hand, gathering data without an idea of what we seek to validate or falsify, can be wasteful.

Success metrics are a good way to define what we want to achieve, based on our capacity/capability. The core DNA of the business teams determines whether we put out bold, ambitious success metrics and the necessary operations to ensure that we deliver them. We also need to track our progress in meeting those success metrics.

There are two key phases of a feature idea (or product) where data-driven decision-making is crucial. The first phase is before we start to build a feature idea and second is after we have launched the feature idea. The type validation we seek at each stage can vary. In the first phase (before we build), we try to validate whether our assumptions about the impact that we expect our feature to have, hold good. In the second (after we launch), we try to measure how well our product is performing on the success metrics. Let's explore more about these two phases of data collection.

#1 – data we need before we build the feature idea

In *Chapter 3*, *Identifying the Solution and its Impact on Key Business Outcomes*, we discussed how to derive impact scores for a feature idea. For impact on Key Business Outcomes that was rated to be more than 5 on a 0-10 scale, we came up with detailed success metrics, but how did stakeholders arrive at this rating? What made them decide to rate an idea as having an impact of 2 on one Key Business Outcome and 8 on another? Was it a gut feeling? Well, it is not entirely a bad idea to go with our gut feeling. There are always situations where we don't have data or there is no existing reference. So, we are essentially placing a bet on the success of the feature idea being able to meet our Key Business Outcomes.

However, we cannot presume that this gut feeling is right and jump straight into building the feature. It is important to step back and analyze if there are ways in which we could find indicators that point us toward the accuracy or inaccuracy of our gut feeling. We need to find ways by which we can validate the core assumptions we're making about the impact a feature will have on Key Business Outcomes, without building the product or setting up elaborate operations. They could be small experiments that we can run to test some hypotheses without spending our resources. I refrain from using the term Minimum Viable Product here, because in many cases, technology or business viability isn't what we're going after. These experiments are more about getting a pulse of the market. They are sort of similar to putting up posters about a movie to tease the interest of the audience, before really making the movie itself.

We can activate the interest of our target group by introducing pricing plans with the proposed feature included in a bundle and excluded in a different one. We could see if customers show an interest in our new feature or not. We can also try out teaser campaigns, landing pages with sign up options , and so on, to see whether the feature piques our customers' interests, and also whether they are willing to pay for such a feature. Problem interviews with a targeted group of customers can also be a useful input to this. For instance, let's say ArtGalore seeks to find out if introducing a gift-wrapping option will result in increased purchases of artworks during the festival season in India. We can add content to the ArtGalore website introducing the concept of gifting artworks for the festive season, and track number of views, clicks , and so on. The entire gifting experience and the end-to-end process need not be built or thought through until we know that there is enough interest from customers.

A big advantage of product experiments, especially in software, is that we can be Agile. We have the opportunity to make minor tweaks quickly, run multiple experiments in parallel, and respond fast to what we're observing. This allows us to conserve our resources and direct them toward the things that are working for us.

We need to figure out the best way to validate our bets, but what doesn't work in the early stages of a product, may work well in a later stage of maturity. What works well with early adopters, may not work well with a scaling consumer base. What works in one demography, may not work for another. If we choose to hold onto our opinions without an open mind, we're in for trouble.

Agility and learnability are key when we're figuring out how to survive. Having a testable hypothesis is about validating our riskiest proposition. If our hypothesis is falsified, then it's time to pivot (if the feature idea is core to the business model, or not, then add it to the product backlog). As author Ash Maurya puts it, "Life is too short to build something that nobody wants." We can keep our product backlog lean by adding only those feature ideas that have the backing of early validation metrics.

#2 – data we need after we launch a feature

Once we launch a feature, we also need to measure and track how our product responds under different scenarios. We defined success metrics to validate the bets we made about the feature idea's impact on Key Business Outcomes. While we check these metrics, we are also evaluating other limitations of our product. Does our product still work well when there is a surge in demand? How does our app respond to peak time demand? What if the peak demand period shifts? What if a new consumer base is adapting our product? Does our product work well in a different geography?

These are ongoing health checks that are needed to ensure that our product continues to deliver and drive value to the consumer and to the business. The data that we gather when a feature is live will be useful in the next phase of product building. If the product performance is stopping us from meeting customer demand, then this is an important input for stakeholders when they decide which Key Business Outcome to invest in. These metrics not only help us respond to change but also to enhance our product's capabilities and identify its limitations. Individual health metrics may not provide ample data that could drive a decision to pivot. However, they may over time provide ample data points to unearth trends, bottlenecks, and strengths. They may also help us to understand the success or failure of an individual feature. Databases, user interaction analytics, volume and performance tracking tools, and so on, can be part of our data strategy to capture and analyze data and trends over time.

The problem with data

1. **Accessing data**: One of the bottlenecks with data (or information) is that it is usually hoarded. Access to data is often limited to technology/data teams or to a few exclusive users. So, stakeholders come to depend on the technology/data teams to provide them with data. They raise requests for data or reports, which data teams provide based on how much time they have to hand. The data/ technology teams make decisions on the fly about when to share data, who to share data with, and in what formats to share the data. When a more powerful stakeholder requests data, it is assumed that the need is urgent and data teams may drop everything else and attend to this. When someone not as powerful requests data, teams may deprioritize this task and not respond as swiftly. These requests also come in sporadically, so there could be redundant requests from different teams and so on. Working on these requests takes time and requires that technology/data teams switch context from product development into addressing ad hoc requests. This is one instance of a feature black hole that we saw in *Chapter 10, Eliminating Waste – Don't Build What We Can Buy.*

It is imperative that today's product teams start with a data mindset. Data strategy and accessibility must be built into a product team's DNA. We cannot assume that we will handle this if the need arises. In many cases, stakeholders don't know the power of data until we show them. Stakeholders also hold themselves back from seeking data because the process of getting data is hard and cumbersome, especially when it feels like they are imposing on the technology team's time. So, it becomes a Catch 22. Technology teams don't build a data strategy because they don't see stakeholders asking for data. Stakeholders don't ask for data because there isn't an easy way to access data.

Product strategy must proactively think, plan, and set up ways to collect data and share data transparently without elaborate procedures. The discussion on success metrics is a good indicator for the type of Key Performance Indicators that should be captured. An effective data strategy sometimes doesn't even need complicated digital tools to capture data. Simple paper-based observations are sometimes enough. Key metrics around revenue, acquisitions, sales , and so on. can even be shared on a whiteboard with a person assigned exclusively to doing this. This works in a small team with an early stage product, but finding digital tools in the market that allow real-time visualization isn't very hard either.

2. **Running incorrect experiments**: In the nonprofit organization where I worked, the finance team wanted us to build an ability for our investors to be able to donate or invest money every month in the rural borrowers listed on our platform. The problem was that investments/donations were sporadic. There was no way to predict how many investors would invest every month. So, because the investment amount was not predictable, we could not determine how many borrowers we should be onboarding. Indian businesses (with the exception of a few utility services) do not have the ability to automatically bill credit cards. So, our best option to get consent once and receive money automatically was to set up monthly direct auto-debits from bank accounts. However, the banks required paperwork to be signed and submitted before enabling this.

The finance team was convinced that investors were not investing every month because we hadn't made this process easier for investors. The product team was asked to pick up on this as a priority, and we started designing the feature. We soon realized that this was a huge feature to implement (purely based on the amount of complexity of rolling this out, and the dependencies on banks to deliver this successfully). We didn't have to estimate story points to figure out how big this was. Also, the paperwork aspect was a government regulation and outside of our control. So, while we could build requests for auto-debits into the workflow of the product, the paperwork still had to be done.

The team was getting pressurized into delivering this, so we started to gather some data. Why did the finance team think this feature would be so impactful in ensuring predictable monthly investments? The finance team insisted that every single customer they had spoken to wanted this option. Now, 100% of consumers wanting to invest every month is too compelling to ignore. Everyone in the leadership team was now convinced that implementing this feature was crucial for us to get repeat investments. Yet as we dug deeper and looked at our data, we found out that we had a very miniscule percentage of our investors who were investing through direct bank debits. The finance team had apparently spoken to only 15 people over the past three months. In a consumer base of over 9000 folks, 15 (the numbers are only indicative and not actuals) was not a sample big enough to base our product decisions on. Essentially, this was a decision not based on facts, but more on an opinion arising out of a limited context. Did it make sense for us to invest in a feature that was impacting so few of our consumers? If all our investors, who were investing through other payment options, such as credit cards, debit cards, and payment wallets, had to transition into paying through auto-debit, it presented a huge operational burden for us, given the paperwork involved. It was clear that given our finance team's capacity, this was not doable.

Once we had invalidated the basis on which the impact on business outcomes had been made, we ran a new experiment. We were now trying to validate if our investors (who were investing through other payment options such as credit cards, debit cards, and payment wallets) were even inclined to invest in us every month. If so, how many such investors were ready?

We built something very simple to validate this. We introduced an option for users to tell us whether they wanted a reminder service that would nudge them to invest in rural entrepreneurs every month. It took us half a day to add this option to our investment workflow. If they chose this option, we informed them that we hadn't yet built the feature and thanked them for helping us to improve our product. After three months of observation, we found that ~12% (the numbers are only indicative and not actuals) of the consumer base (who transacted on our website) opted in.

This was a big improvement from our earlier target base. While it was a good enough indicator and worth exploring we were still limited by our ability to automatically charge credit cards. So, we limited our solution to a reminder service to send out automated emails on specific dates to the customers who had opted in for a re-investment and tracked conversions from those. We explored our data to see if there was a trend in investments peaking on certain days/dates each month. We found that data trends indicated certain dates when there was a peak in investment. We scheduled our reminder emails to be sent on the peak investment date of each month.

After three months of observing conversions from reminder emails, we figured that this strategy was working well enough for us. We continued to sign up more investors and to socialize the payment reminder on our website.

3. **Learning from the wrong data**: What if we have compelling data, but our data is flawed in how we chose to collect it? Design has a great influence on how people use products, for instance, using coercive design versus persuasive design. These concepts boil down to simple things such as which option presented to the user is checked by default. If we choose to select an option to donate $1 to charity by default, and we keep it hidden at the bottom of a page, where no user has seen it, then we can't claim that visitors to our website are very generous.

Basing product decisions on data alone is not enough. It is necessary to collect ample verifiable evidence, but it is also important to capture this data at a time when the consumer is in the right context. For instance, asking for feedback on a website's payment process two weeks after a customer purchased something trivial, may not work very well. Context, timing, content, and sample size are key to finding data that is relevant for use.

4. **Bias**: Gathering data is only half the battle. Interpreting data is the dangerous other half. Human cognitive biases form a big part of the incorrect decisions that we make based on data. We feel great that we have used data to base our decisions on, which means that we don't even recognize the inherent biases we bring into making our decisions.

For instance, my biases influence how I configure my social feeds. I found that a lot of content on my feeds was not appealing to my tastes or opinions. I started unfollowing a lot of people. I got picky about the groups and people I followed. Voilà, my social feed was suddenly palatable and full of things I wanted to hear.

This personal bias could potentially trickle into how we make recommendations on product platforms. We make recommendations of songs/movies/products/blogs based on our consumer's own likes and dislikes. This means that we are essentially appealing to the confirmation bias of our consumers. The more content we show them that appeals to their existing interests, the more likely they will be to engage with us. This shows us a positive trend in our engagement rates, and our recommendation strategy gets further strengthened. In the long run, though, we are slowly but silently creating highly opinionated individuals who have very little tolerance for anything but their own preferences.

Whether this is good or bad for business is dependent on the business intent itself. However, the bigger question to ask is: how do we learn something new about our customers, if we don't go beyond their current preferences?

Our bias also influences how we interpret data. For example, we might start with a hypothesis that women don't apply for core technology jobs. This might mean that our ads, websites, and social content have nothing that appeals to women. Yet, if the messaging and imagery on our careers website is well-attuned to middle-aged men in white-collar jobs, then can we claim that we can't find women who are qualified to work with us? Does this prove our hypothesis correct?

Summary

In this chapter, we found out that formulating an effective data strategy right from the start can help businesses to build a healthy data culture. Product decisions and priorities can be made objectively. We can eliminate waste in our data strategy by following some simple tactics:

1.   Defining what to validate

2.   Defining our success metrics

3.   Digging deeper into data that sounds like facts, but is actually only opinions

We now have a lean product backlog and data to back up our success metrics. In the next chapter, we will figure out if our team processes are slowing us down from delivering the Impact Driven Product.

~12~

IS OUR PROCESS DRAGGING US DOWN?

Product teams need the ability to respond swiftly to feedback from the market and the changing business landscape. In order to respond swiftly, we need to structure our processes to our way of working. This means that we need to be prudent about setting up processes based on our resources, assessing where to optimize our processes and ensuring we set up our delivery based on time to market. This chapter addresses the typical process bottlenecks, followed by a recommendation for each.

The reasons for process waste include the following:

- Striving for perfection
- Striving for efficiency
- Striving for throughput

Business and organization context

"A chain is only as strong as its weakest link."

During my tenure at a software consultancy organization, I was part of a team that consulted for a nonprofit organization running a small t-shirt and bag manufacturing factory. The organization employed rehabilitated sex workers (who had been forced into the sex trade), trained them, and offered them an opportunity to earn a living. The organization wanted us to evaluate if a technology solution could help with their operations and manufacturing pipeline. We spent a day learning about each step of their process and talking to the women working in each section of the factory.

I clearly recall one of the problems that they brought to our attention. The bag production process involved many steps. It started with receiving bales of cloth, which then had to be cut based on the orders required. Once the bags had gone through stitching, quality checks, and printing, they would all be packed into batches of 50 bags. Another group of workers would count each pack and if there was a mismatch, the batch would be flagged. However, the workers who were packing bags in each batch were a group of older women. They didn't have the skills or the strength to handle any of the key tailoring activities, but the nonprofit organization wanted to help them to make a living. So, this part of the process (counting bags and putting them into boxes) was thought to be the most suitable for these women.

A key problem here was that the women were uneducated and didn't know how to count! So, every once in a while, a batch had a couple of bags over or under the specified count. Now, to identify these irregular batches someone had to recount every bag! The organization had tried to train these women to count, but it can be quite hard to learn when you're over 60 years of age. It was also demoralizing for the older women that someone had to re-do what they had already done. Solving the bag counting bottleneck was becoming tricky. No matter how fast the team went in the manufacturing process, the last step was slowing down the organization when it was trying to pack and ship orders on time. The organization wanted us to suggest a digital solution to this (along with the other bottlenecks they were facing elsewhere in their processes).

We recommended a simple solution: we asked the organization to try putting together a sample reference batch, with 50 bags, and had the team weigh it. Once the weight was noted, we asked them to try weighing every batch that was counted, and verified by the older women against this weight just before packing. This was a faster process, and the organization could now easily separate the batches with too many or too few bags and fix those only. The younger women, who packed the cartons with finished batches, could do this check, and it wouldn't delay them much. Now, I don't know whether they pursued this approach or not, but it did open their minds to the possibility that they could look for alternate approaches to solving problems.

If our team hadn't known the context behind the organization, we may have suggested replacing the bag counting team with better-educated women or finding alternative digital solutions to this. Even a simple counting ticker could have been proposed, but given how hard it was to train the women, and knowing that the organization's prime goal was rehabilitation, we suggested the simplest thing to address the issue at hand.

In our pursuit for optimizing everything, we tend to forget that people are central to what we do. The internal dynamics of how our teams work determine how well we can collaboratively contribute value. Setting up a process and then forcing people to follow it is usually ineffective. It is also ineffective to set up a process once and assume that we're set for life. People and context should drive processes. Also, processes need to evolve as people do and as the context changes.

What actions we take at the initial stages of a product life cycle cannot be the same as what we do once the product is live and has a thriving consumer base. Internal motivations, needs, and maybe even culture, all drive how teams work and co-ordinate with others. However, process wastes can weigh heavily on our ability to deliver product value.

As mentioned at the start of the chapter, at a broad level, there are three reasons why process wastes (activities that consume our resources, but create no value for the customers) creep in: striving for perfection, striving for efficiency, and striving to maximize throughput. Strangely, these goals don't seem like bad things to strive for. Yet, they can be quite counterproductive to how we build and launch products.

Reason #1 for process waste – striving for perfection

Taking a product from poor to good requires effort. For this, we need to validate customer pain points, validate the problem-solution fit, and find a model to monetize our solution. Taking a product from good to great requires a different level of effort. We need to find the best offering that can deliver the most impactful end-to-end experience and meet our Key Business Outcomes. However, trying to take a product from great to *perfect* can be so hard that it actually slows us down. It's not due to lack of talent, time, or resources. It's mostly because no one knows what perfect is. *Perfection* sometimes is only an aspirational state. It exists only in our minds.

A typical situation that I have faced in many teams is where we depend on one person's final go-ahead before we release anything to production. This happens in spite of set processes in teams where scope had been agreed upon, designs had been iterated and finalized, and code had been tested to meet acceptance criteria. An hour before launch, the founder, CEO, product head, or key business stakeholder would appear dissatisfied with the visual appeal of a product. You would hear stuff like, "This is not giving a wow effect," or "This is not quite what I was expecting." These kinds of comments could stall everything. Such feedback is neither constructive nor SMART. Additionally, in their endeavor to guide to us toward what will 'wow them,' we end up getting bogged down by opinions, and inspirational examples instead of specific, data-driven insights.

This kind of situation throws teams off balance. The feedback that comes from an important stakeholder carries a lot of weight. Differentiating between an opinion and constructive, actionable feedback, backed by data, is a necessary skill to master, as we discussed in *Chapter 11, Eliminate Waste – Data Versus Opinions*. Still, teams can do nothing even when they know that what they are hearing is an opinion that an influential stakeholder formed by seeing a shiny new idea somewhere. In trying to even find the rationale behind deciding between pursuing or not pursuing the new idea/ recommendation/feedback, teams are using quality time that should be spent building something of value.

Striving for perfection can make us obsessed over details that may not create any additional value for the customer, but serve only to feed our egos. We cannot afford to lose sight of the larger objective of getting the product released. It becomes imperative for the main stakeholders to hold themselves accountable for their feedback. If the main stakeholder reluctantly agrees to release the product as is, and then at every opportunity, makes it a point to let the team know that they should have listened to their opinions or indicates that the product could have been so much better had they followed their last-minute vague inputs, it can create great reluctance in the team to ever want to release anything without approval from the stakeholder.

Amazon's CEO, Jeff Bezos, in his letter to his shareholders, talks about "disagree and commit." He refers to high-velocity decision-making and says, "If you're good at course correcting, being wrong may be less costly than you think, whereas being slow is going to be expensive for sure."

For a business to be able to put out an Impact Driven Product, the intent at every stage of decision-making must be to move forward and not stall. To pursue one person's idea of perfection cannot be the prerogative for the product. Teams and leaders must be able to let go of personal opinions and instead focus on the larger goal. Once a decision is taken, teams must commit to enabling the success of the decision. It must not become a team's primary job to convince the stakeholders on every decision about the product. Stakeholders must be accountable and must enable teams to take the product ahead and commit to deliver based on the what we know today. They must be open to course correction as they discover new data. When we do not launch our product and keep improving our product based on every new input we receive, we are missing out on a huge opportunity to learn from our customers and market conditions that are relevant to the nature of our business.

This pursuit of perfection, as an ever-changing goal post, can be counterproductive. It reinforces a cycle of dependency, where the key stakeholders hold the reins on the minute details of the product, and the team is unwilling to proceed without their approval. So how can we fix this tendency to overengineer, and the desire to design for every edge case, and to fix every defect, without understanding the larger context? Let's dwell on this for a moment and think about the other reasons for process wastes in our teams. The solutions to eliminating these process wastes form the latter half of this chapter.

Reason #2 for process waste – striving for efficiency

Early-stage start-ups may not have well-defined product teams. Everyone does everything and there are no clear boundaries on roles or responsibilities. However, as the business grows, there is a need to focus on specific areas. This is where streamlining begins. Specialist roles become necessary. This also leads to silos getting created, where each specialization takes off on its own path, which can result in less coordination. When there is less coordination between different streams, shared business context is also compromised.

This can be quite hard to see happening, since each specialization is often tuned to work efficiently. Their efficiency breaks down only when they have to coordinate with other teams. For instance, marketing teams may have great synergies amongst themselves, but when they require assistance from engineering, they may find that the response is slow. This is because the engineering team has set its own priorities and has to handle requests from other teams as well. Since marketing and engineering are not working under the same context and toward the same priorities, there is friction. Each team now feels that they are being slowed down by the other team.

Even within product engineering teams, we're likely to see this. For instance, data (business intelligence and data engineering) is a specialization, but it is relevant for many streams of a product, as is TechOps.

However, data and TechOps have their own priorities, which could suffer because of incoming requests from other teams. We discussed in *Chapter 11, Eliminate Waste – Data Versus Opinions,* the catch-22 situation that happens when the data strategy is kept inaccessible to the organization and the data team becomes a bottleneck in reporting data to teams when they need it.

This is a bottleneck that we have created by striving for efficiency through streamlining. Streamlining has its advantages: there is better focus and speed, and also, less distractions from other operational functions. However, the disadvantage is the lack of context. Due to this lack of context, each team tends to further increase their own efficiency by creating better tracking mechanisms, and more processes, but in silos. This results in higher frustration and distrust among teams since no matter how efficient they try to be, other teams always disrupt their well-oiled processes.

Another glaring result of streamlining is the broken experience for the customer. All of us have likely seen some variant of this. When we buy a product (say, a car), we are welcomed by a sales person, who gives personal attention to us and assures us of the best quality and price. Once the sale is done, the sales person is out of the picture. Other functions take over. Billing, delivery, and customer support treat us very differently. We have come to rationalize this, saying, "After all, they have their money from me now." Very often, different departments aren't connected and this issue can even be seen within customer service teams. When talking to support folks at call centers, if they transfer our call to a supervisor, or to another agent, we have to repeat ourselves all over again. Each person we talk to has to be able to understand our context. The onus is placed on the customer to do this.

In order to get an overarching view of our individual functions, we end up creating program management roles. We think we need one person, or team, that oversees coordination between individual functions. By doing this, we will have shifted the problem from the individual teams to a different group, which has the responsibility of managing inter-team coordination, but has no accountability in delivery. Now what? Again, let's dwell on this for a moment and jump to our third reason for process waste. The solution to this is in the latter half of this chapter.

Reason #3 for process waste – striving to maximize throughput

Writing code is not the same as fitting nuts and bolts onto car parts. It is not a mechanical skill. It does not involve repetitive actions. Building great software requires creativity. Yet, we are so keen to pursue processes influenced by manufacturing paradigms. The lean principles outlined in Mary and Tom Poppendieck's book *Lean Software Development*, have been widely interpreted and applied without context to software development. Even the Kanban method (which is essentially a way of managing the supply of components in Japanese manufacturing based on pull or capacity to work) can rarely be applied to the context of software development without sufficiently modifying the paradigms to suit the nature of software development itself.

Manufacturing deals with repetitive tasks, equal-sized chunks of work and supply and demand that can be predicted/tweaked based on trends and optimizing process scheduling, assembly line structures , and so on. The question is, what do we gain by measuring throughput (amount of work done in a given cycle/period of time) in software product development?

> *"When a measure becomes a target, it ceases to be a good measure."*
> *- Goodhart's Law*

An often-quoted example of Goodhart's Law is about the nail factories in the Soviet Union. When the factories were given a target, based on the number of nails manufactured, the operators produced plenty of tiny nails. When targets were based on the weight of nails produced, operators produced heavy nails. In both cases, the nails were useless! With software this gets even trickier. There are some parts which are very automation-friendly (repeatable and rule-based), while there are others where creativity and ingenuity matter a lot. *Throughput* measurement only makes sense when you want to reliably predict *when things will be done*. This is possible only when there is some aspect of repeatability.

In a similar way to the Soviet nail factories, I have heard quality analysts in software teams tell stories about how their performance appraisal was based on the number of defects found. They would then go about finding every sort of defect. Instead of working with the developers to try and find solutions to deliver value, the focus was on maximizing bug counts.

Can we measure throughput for creative, artistic ventures? I can best explain this based on my artistic interludes with painting. Painting requires some preparation, such as choosing the right paints and material, getting brushes ready, priming canvases, and so on. Then there is the creative part of painting itself. The preparation part is repeatable and can be handed off to someone with no artistic skills too. It can be done by a robot. I can more or less predict my *cycle time* in the preparation part. However, if you attempt to predict how long I will take to complete my painting, you're bound to fail. Even if you have all the data about my past paintings and how long I took to complete each of them, there is a big variable that you cannot account for: me.

Even when the technique of painting can be taught, the creativity and flair is highly influenced by the artist's personality. For instance, when I am in the groove, I paint with much speed and abandon. When I am not, I may be slow and deliberate, or I may churn up strokes that need a rework or I might just start all over. There are phases in the painting when I have to be slow and deliberate, especially with the finishing touches. There are then phases when unrestrained creativity must take over.

Choosing the painting media can also be very personality-centric. The media (for example, paints) that we choose and how well we work with them, can depend on our personality. I tend to experiment with a lot of media — acrylics, water colors, oil and charcoal. Each medium has a characteristic, in terms of how pliable it is, how soon it dries, how much control we have over the medium , and so on. For instance, oil, paints are extremely pliable and so they are wonderful to work with, but they can take forever to dry. Acrylics, on the other hand, dry fast and they are somewhat pliable like oils. Now, the medium that I choose and my personality sort of decide how long I will take to paint, and also how I want to plan my paintings. I know for sure that I cannot predict my *cycle time* when painting.

"Painting is easy when you don't know how, but very difficult when you do."
— *Edgar Degas*

Software development is not very different from producing a painting. There are aspects that are repeatable and need technique, which can be taught. There are also aspects that require expertise, creativity, and flair. While some ideas from process optimizations in manufacturing can apply to software, we need to be cognizant that software development is largely a creative field. There are small pockets of repetitive work, and those can be automated. For instance, regression testing of an application can be automated. However, measuring throughput from a regression testing suite is as absurd as measuring throughput from a software developer writing code for a custom business need.

There are phases where you should build with abandon. There are also phases where you should be slow and deliberate. All of this should work in tandem, and with great orchestration among dissimilar personalities. People bring relationships, trust, and personality to a team. There's no framework to predict how passionate, creative people can make magic. There's no magic pill that can measure human potential with numbers and graphs. Any process framework that treats its teams as less human will always fall flat on its face. Undermining people will get us 'hands on board', but not commitment.

The core Agile principles capture the essence of this: "Individuals and interactions over processes and tools." However, we have translated that into frameworks that have created meaningless processes and tools. A process framework should be for organizing stuff, not for predicting people or measuring productivity. Typically, throughput measurement is needed when we want to accurately predict *when* we can deliver a piece of work. We have become quite adept at defining our piece of work in terms of user stories and comparing the size of user stories in terms of story points. However, in software development, the specific team context, business/technology domain, culture, and individual personalities can have a bearing on how soon or late a piece of work can be delivered. Two user stories estimated to be 'small' are comparable, but are not the same. They may or may not take the same time to build.

Even the same story, if developed by another developer, could take less or more time. In a setup where budgets and scope are fixed, knowing how long it would take to develop the given scope, without burning budget, is important. For instance, software consultancies and services may need to justify *throughput*, in terms of working software delivered versus hours clocked, especially when in a time and materials contract. Hence, the emphasis on velocity, iterations, cycle time, time sheet management, and so on.

Today, even consultancies are moving away from time and budget-based models to outcome-based, income-sharing type models, where human productivity is no longer measured by number of hours clocked, but by the value of the product that has been created. So, in products where the scope is evolving based on customer/market demands, and budgets are decided based on the business' capacity to make revenue or raise investments, the emphasis should be less about time taken to build, and more about the impact that we can create. The smarter we are about delivering impact, the easier it is to move forward as a business. We need to recognize that measuring throughput isn't the best use of a product team's time. Throughput indicators don't matter for products. Outcome indicators do.

So, why should product teams have any process that measures *throughput*? Now that we have outlined the three basic reasons for process wastes, let's look at some solutions for tackling each reason discussed above.

Solutions to eliminating process waste

Most of what has been described earlier happens because it's hard to take a big picture view on processes as we evolve as a business. We fall back into the "we have always done it this way" mode and try to adapt *best practices* and apply them to our context. We set up story boards, have stand ups, estimate stories, measure velocity, and reward bug finders. It has worked for us in the past, or everyone says it has worked, so we believe that it can't hurt us. This seems natural. However, what we may need is a new set of *best practices* that can help teams to navigate the ambiguous phases when there is no luxury to customize processes. When you do have the luxury, I strongly suggest that you tune your processes around the specific goals, culture and needs of your teams. The following are the new process guidelines that I would recommend.

Solution #1 – don't strive for perfection, instead set up outcome-driven timelines

> *"You can't just turn on creativity like a faucet. You have to be in the right mood...last-minute panic!" Calvin and Hobbes, Bill Waterson*

Constraints have a great way of bringing focus to work. They have also been shown to have an effect on creativity. Having unlimited options and possibilities, in fact, makes it harder for us to make decisions (decision fatigue). When we create a product plan, we are dealing with a number of options and have many decisions to take. These can range from something as high level as what feature to build, to something as finely detailed as where to place the purchase button.

When faced with so many decisions, and many of them being in the speculative zone, setting up a constraint can help to bring focus. Time is a clear, tangible constraint that has an intense effect on our psyche. Time lost cannot be recovered, but our tendency is to keep extending time. If we're not ready, then we say, "Let's give it another day." If we find something new and cool, then we say, "Let's take time to explore and retrofit to our product." So, we grant ourselves the liberty to bring in last-minute changes. We let ourselves obsess over details, which may not be critical to the product.

If there is one discipline that we should incorporate into our product cycle, then it is to keep time (deadlines) as a non-negotiable aspect. This is probably raising the eyebrows of folks who would rightly argue that it will lead to overworking, 24/7 schedules, and a lack of time for personal life. However, that's where the fine line comes between someone dictating a deadline and a team finding a timeline based on desired outcomes. In some cases, when demanded by the market, release dates may not even be in our control. We have to launch when we have to launch. For instance, if you're selling diyas (lights) for Diwali, then you can't wait until Christmas to make your diyas. So, we must take into account either market priorities (launching ahead of a competitor or in time for the festival season) or internal consensus to set a date (we will launch on October 7th, one week before Diwali), or a schedule (we will release updates every Tuesday or we will release them every day). We need to strive to meet outcome-driven timelines.

Now, we must make every decision with the intent to meet the outcome-driven timeline. Any obsession about details that will make us miss the deadline is not worth it. Any last-minute changes that will delay our launch must be rationalized and justified, backed with data, and have a compelling reason. Otherwise, we go with what was agreed upon. There is much more to learn from how the customer adopts our product than we will ever learn from our own opinions of what's the best product to build. So, getting the product out of the door should be our intent. Setting time-bound outcome goals will create that focus, and discipline, for us.

In the classic iron triangle of scope, budget, and time, when time is fixed, there is limited flexibility to increase scope or budget. Since budget is already spent, and because of Brooks' law ("Adding human resources to a late software project makes it later"), any tweaking on budget is out of the question:

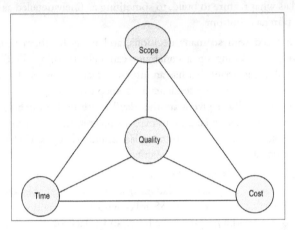

So that leaves scope. When forced by the constraints of meeting a non-negotiable date, scope prioritization becomes very creative. We critically evaluate every change request, and every functional aspect. It becomes much easier to identify things that need to go into a product by that launch date, things which can be pushed to later, and things we shouldn't even be building. Question every change in scope by asking, "Is adding this scope worth missing the deadline?"

Let me recall an incident narrated by a friend on her experience with time-bound goals. Her team was gearing up to build an online e-commerce platform for niche handicrafts made by women who ran small home businesses. Right from the start, they had tried to match up with every functionality that platforms such as Magento, WooCommerce, or Shopify offered. There had been a lack of focus due to many competing priorities, since they wanted to build everything under the sun. The team continued to build without focus, until there was a sudden deadline imposed due to pressure from investors. They had to go live in two weeks.

With two weeks to go, the product lead threw up his arms in despair. Many functional flows were incomplete. No one had tested anything. Panic set in! The first instinct was for everyone to request that they move the launch date because we were not ready. Yet the investors did not relent and the team was forced to evaluate how they could meet the deadline. The net result was that the team mercilessly cut down scope, looked at the key outcomes that the investors were looking for, and identified the critical functionality that could best meet those outcomes within the time constraints.

Having unlimited time wasn't really helping the team. Even though a two-week timeline may not have been the optimal time needed to carve out the Impact Driven Product, the point is that a constraint like that forces teams to evaluate and redirect all their resources to meeting an outcome, under the given constraints. The constraint of time is great antidote for teams that strive for perfection.

Solution #2 – don't strive for efficiency, instead foster collaboration

Smaller teams, with a narrower focus of responsibility, may be able to deliver better results. This happens due to lesser distractions, clarity in objectives, and higher team coordination. However, as explained earlier, teams can get too focused on their internal priorities, and lose track of the larger context. We also discussed how adding a program management overhead, to solve cross-team coordination, only adds to the chaos, since program management has responsibility without accountability.

When there is responsibility without accountability, it causes a mismatch in expectations. Managers can choose to get things done in areas where they have better control, because it makes them succeed with little effort. It helps them to check things off the to-do list, whether or not there is value delivered. However, because they have no accountability, when there is a delay, the tendency is to blame people or to optimize productivity. It also causes managers to prefer folks who say yes to everything, and not respond to the folks who offer rational justification for delays. In addition to this cultural side effect, this results in poor value for the end consumer too, since we are focused on delivering output and not on delivering impact.

Streamlining can create focus, but it also creates a broken experience for the customer. One effective way to solve this is to set up cross-functional teams or at a bare minimum have cross-functional interactions. Let's say that the product team is trying to build an email notification to send to users on their first time signing up. Making the email work is only part of the solution. The content of the email (what information we tell the consumer on sign-up) may need input from marketing and sales or business development. In case of issues, coordination from customer support is needed. If we think about an email notification as a technical problem to solve and fill it with half-thought-out content, then we aren't doing any justice to the customer experience. We might think that we will reach out to marketing or support when we need their input, but that's not always possible.

So, instead of creating two teams with a narrow functional focus and adding a communication overhead, we need to create cross-functional teams:

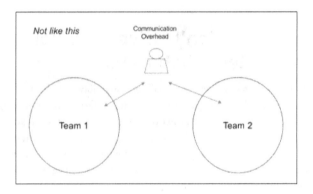

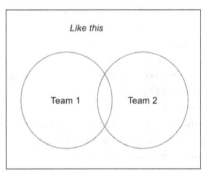

As shown in the preceding diagrams, instead of making cross-team communication the responsibility of one person, we need to make cross-team collaboration the norm. Some ways in which we can achieve this are as follows:

- Investing in Key Business Outcomes must have consensus and representation from every business function.
- Success metrics for feature ideas are agreed upon and owned by respective business functions
- Set up daily stand ups/check-ins that involve at least one member from each team. The intent should be to identify blockers, dependencies, and progress.

While each team can continue to work on their area of expertise, they should be expected to contribute to and be aware of other team's priorities, and no team should be working on anything other than what is needed to meet the outcome-driven timelines. This eliminates the need for external coordination, and also reduces rework and missed opportunities, and improves focus on the consumer experience. So, instead of striving for efficiency through streamlining, we should strive for consistency in user experience across team functions.

Solution #3 – don't strive for throughput, instead restructure teams based on outcome-driven timelines

Releasing often helps us to learn and respond swiftly to feedback, but how often is often? A combination of timeline, effort, and desired outcomes (business and customer impact) may determine how often we release. Some functionality can be built in a few hours. Some can take a few days or weeks. Also, based on the stage of product maturity, we may need less or more focus on technical stability. Technical success criteria are likely to vary based on desired outcomes. Customer context and market needs also have a bearing on how soon or frequently we can update our product.

If something can be released in a few hours and can speed up our feedback cycle, then why wait until the end of day? If something can be released in a day, then why wait until the weekly release cycle? Part of this is how development and production environments are set up, or how code pipelines are structured and so on, but there is also a process component to this.

I have faced these issues in many of the organizations where I have worked. In one instance, I was part of the team that was developing the retail website for a brand. Once the core website was launched, the team's time was split between building new features, fixing defects, and responding to constant requests from customer communications about changing mailer content or website redesigns, or creating new campaigns based on the marketing needs for that week. The team had been following regular monthly releases during the development of the website. They continued to follow their monthly release cycle even after the launch. This meant that communications and marketing had to structure their work around the product team's monthly release cycles. This constantly frustrated them, since it greatly reduced their flexibility for running weekly campaigns.

The product team was fighting off ad hoc requests. It was like they were forever saying no to every request. By the time a monthly release came, some of these requests were missed out, or had escalated. On the other hand, the team was also responding to production support requests. Again, in the absence of a data-based approach, an influential customer's trivial request was being prioritized over a recurring pattern of critical requests from various users. Since the team was switching context between support hot fixes, marketing support and feature enhancements, they dropped the ball quite often. The impression that management had was that the product team was not productive enough.

We then decided to investigate how we could solve this problem. We reviewed the data of all the requests they had worked on for the past three months. We noticed a pattern in terms of the time spent by the team across various activities. We then did something counter-intuitive: we restructured the team based on the swiftness of the response required.

We figured that production support required swift action, but also needed sufficient product context and the mindset to investigate impact. Regular marketing and communications needed quick turnaround and Agility, but not a great level of technical expertise. Product building needed a balance of sound technical expertise and product context. Some features needed quick turnaround and Agility. Some others needed strategic, long-term solutioning.

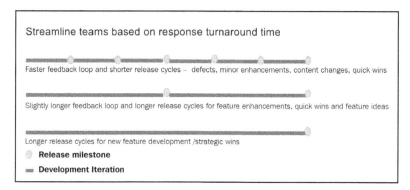

Streamline teams based on response turnaround time

Faster feedback loop and shorter release cycles – defects, minor enhancements, content changes, quick wins

Slightly longer feedback loop and longer release cycles for feature enhancements, quick wins and feature ideas

Longer release cycles for new feature development /strategic wins

- Release milestone
- Development Iteration

So, the teams organized themselves into smaller groups based on response cycles and outcomes. We also set up smaller cross-functional groups based on the outcomes. For instance, communications and marketing representatives would have a daily check-in with a couple of members from the product team, who owned the delivery of shorter release cycles. They could track and plan their work based on the pace at which they needed to respond to requests/feedback or new feature idea development. For this, we also had to structure product backlog requests, release pipelines and so on. The key outcome from this restructuring was that the team could now work without distractions, and by having created subteams, based on the speed of response required, we had managed to remove a big bottleneck. Each of the preceding solutions are only indicative and intended to serve as a guideline in the absence of other indicators. In essence though, every team would benefit by assessing their specific needs and creating processes around their needs, rather than following a standard process.

Summary

In this chapter, we discovered that product teams must evaluate what process wastes are consuming their time and taking them away from delivering impact. Our focus must always be on delivering impact and we need to optimize our processes in a way that's best suited to meeting internal and external constraints. After all, there is no value in following processes and best practices and delivering a product that creates no impact for the business or for the customer.

Now that we have seen some solutions to structuring our teams and streamlining our processes, let's explore in the next chapter why team empowerment plays a big part in a team's ability to deliver impact.

~ 13 ~

TEAM EMPOWERMENT

In the early stages of product development, effort is creative, experimental, and iterative. The focus remains on finding the product-market fit. The product must prove that business outcomes of growth, sustainability, and influence are achievable. Product-market fit should define the recipe for what works well for the business, while offering the most value to the customers. In this phase, speed, Agility, focus, decision-making, and team empowerment are essential tenets for organizations. This helps them to stay on course without running out of resources. Product management acts as the orchestrator that enables product development. It can help to amplify impact to meet business outcomes and offer customer value. Yet, there are reasons why teams fail.

This chapter addresses the following topics:

- Tenets of lean software development
- Why team empowerment is essential for building successful products
- Two main aspects of empowered teams

Tenets of lean software development

> *"If you really want to do something, you'll find a way. If you don't, you'll find an excuse."*
>
> *– Jim Rohn*

Mary and Tom Poppendieck, in their book, *Lean Software Development*, lay out a finely compiled guide of the lean principles that can be applied to software development. They rightly caution against the misapplication of manufacturing and civil engineering practices to software development:

> *"Software development has tried to model its practices after manufacturing and civil engineering, with decidedly mixed results. This has been due in part to a naive understanding of the true nature of these disciplines and a failure to recognize the limits of the metaphor."*

As the authors have pointed out in the book, it is this failure to recognize the limits of the metaphor that is prevalent in product teams. The mindset of thinking that software development is akin to manufacturing/production has a huge implication on how teams perceive software practices. We place an inordinately high emphasis on processes. These processes seek to optimize development, treating it as if it is a repeatable task that can follow a spec.

Mary and Tom Poppendieck compare **development** to designing a recipe, where iteration and variability in results are actually value-adds, as opposed to **production**, where variable results are bad, and iterations generate waste. The early stages of product development (preproduct-market fit) require processes, and Agility, suited to development and not production. We're trying to find the right recipe, not produce food for the masses. Not yet! Preproduct-market fit product teams have to be nimble and ready to iterate or throw everything away and start from scratch. We have to try out various experiments in order to find the Most Valuable Product for the consumer. We need to deliver on the business outcomes before we run out of resources. However, there are many reasons why teams fail to find the right balance in how they well they collaborate. This happens even when they intend to be Agile, respond to feedback, have the best interests of the consumer at heart, and are savvy about costs. The key tenets of lean and their counter-patterns, laid out in Mary and Tom Poppendieck's book, are as follows:

- **Eliminate waste** does not mean throw away all documentation
- **Amplify learning** does not mean keep on changing your mind
- **Decide as late as possible** does not mean procrastinate
- **Deliver as fast as possible** does not mean rush and do sloppy work
- **Empower the team** does not mean abandon leadership
- **Build integrity in** does not mean big, upfront design
- **See the whole** does not mean ignore the details

Throughout this book, we have looked at the following:

- **Eliminating wasteful processes** by throwing away processes and metrics relating to team productivity
- **Amplifying our learning** by investing in Key Business Outcomes and defining success metrics upfront so as to learn valuable product insights, and not just fail fast
- **Decide as late as possible** by thinking through build versus buy versus not at all and gathering data to make informed decisions
- **Deliver as fast as possible** by setting up outcome-driven timelines and identifying the smartest way to deliver impact
- **Building integrity in** by ensuring that impact (business outcomes and customer value) remains the key goal of all product development and setting up a data strategy to track, measure, and share product adoption insights
- **Seeing the whole** by defining an Impact Driven Product that ensures that we build an end-to-end product experience, and not just isolated pockets of product efficiency

This book offers a framework for working through the details of the product. We started with the strategic business goals and narrowed them down to the finer details. Product backlog planning and iterating on feedback is reviewed in the context of Key Business Outcomes. While teams can adopt this framework (as I am hopeful you will), teams that are not empowered will find it hard to apply it effectively. I want to place the focus on **empowering the team** from two different aspects. The first is in the context of decision making and the second is in the context of collaboration.

Decision making

When business conditions are fluid and changing, as we uncover fuzzy ideas for the product, we discover more about the factors and variables that affect our business outcomes. Keeping things loosely coupled and flexible can work well in our favor. It can help us to respond to new information better, without being held back by the cost of rework due to choices made previously. If anything, our efforts should be towards getting as much data and upfront analyses as possible. We must think through our options and have a good grasp on the benefits and trade-offs of the options we have, so that when the time to take a decision is nigh, we are well prepared. So, I'm sure we would all agree that in order to make informed decisions better and faster, we need full visibility into all aspects that concern product strategy.

Stakeholders from different businesses and technology functions need to come together to align on strategy. When they do, they must be ready and inclined to share their insights. After all, they have the most visibility about financial status, investment prospects, and the bigger picture. In larger enterprises, where multiple product lines may be spawned, information about budgets, people skills, and sponsorship can influence product strategy. It is quite possible to have frictions between teams within an enterprise, about who owns the product, and who assigns budget and resources. It is also very natural that senior leadership will have to navigate the quagmire of cross-departmental politics and be able to make decisions. The ownership usually lies with them.

A problem occurs when the team that implements a strategy is kept in the dark about these background developments. The general view is that unfavorable or ambiguous business conditions may render the team without direction, affect the team morale, and slow down the team. So, the business sponsors then don't share information that could potentially derail the product, even before it takes off, while misleading the team to chase metrics that don't matter. When data is withheld, partially shared, or shared without context, even the smartest of teams will make suboptimal decisions, based on whatever little they know at the time. However, there is a difference between divulging all details of the political quagmire at the cost of demoralizing the team and divulging enough details to influence the product strategy.

A few years ago, when I was working at a software consultancy company, I was asked to own and drive an internal product targeted at the developer community. Our local office leadership was sponsoring the initiative and gave us a deadline of 4 months to launch the first phase. We knew that a previous attempt at this product had fallen flat. We understood that developers were key to the adoption of the product. A small team of four, we were gearing up to get a buy-in from the developers. We worked closely with them to fine-tune our value proposition. However, every other week, someone from a different department, such as IT security or Tech Ops, would seek to know what we were up to. We started to get requirements from teams which were not even on our radar. By the fourth week, we had no idea how many stakeholders were even involved in the success of the product.

The local office leadership recommended that we get all the known stakeholders together and facilitate a discussion and alignment around the vision for the product. That meeting, unfortunately, ended by being more about pacifying upset stakeholders than about defining the product strategy. We finally did manage to carve out the strategy. Some stakeholders were still hesitant to align on the functionality outlined in the high-level roadmap. While we, the implementation team, were worried about this lack of alignment, the local leadership seemed unconcerned. So, we started to work on the pilot product. We also started to sign up an early adopter group of developers to test it. All this was while we were assuming that this was only a question of alignment on product functionality.

After two months, much to our dismay, the product was scrapped since there was no alignment on budget! All along there had been a tug of war in terms of sponsorship for this product. The local leadership had failed to take the global group into their confidence or partner with them in owning the product strategy. Right from the beginning, the essential aspects of product sponsorship had never been addressed. If anything, that was the riskiest proposition for the venture. We, the executing team, were kept completely in the dark. We had been chasing our tails, trying to rearrange deck chairs on the Titanic!

In an evolving business, product management plays a crucial role in aligning product strategy with business outcomes and delivering the best end-to-end experience for customers. When product teams are kept in the dark about changing business priorities, it can adversely impact product strategy and lead to teams wasting time, effort, and resources building products that the business has no plans to pursue. This book proposes a framework to ensure that we understand business drivers and outcomes we want to place our bets on. However, this framework cannot be effective if key stakeholders want to withhold information about business drivers or mislead teams with namesake investments, while actual business decisions are in a different direction. Teams that take a business vision and convert it into a smart execution plan to deliver value, must always be aligned with the business strategy and direction. This visibility on business alignment is possible only when product teams are empowered to be an integral part of the overall business direction, if not the detailed business strategy.

While this is true in organizations with a 'need to know' culture, we can see the other extreme manifestation in startups with small teams, where openness and access to information is highly valued. The manifestation of the problem here is what I'd call 'death by discussions.' This is when everyone in an organization is treated with equal merit and every opinion is to be valued. This is, of course, such a desirable state for teams to be in, but they spend an enormous amount of time in discussions before arriving at decisions for even the most straightforward of things. This antipattern can adversely affect product progress. After all, when you ask me an opinion, I'll give you two. Involving a diverse group of people, with different experience levels, skills, and expertise, which can open up wonderful ideas and perspectives. Yet, there is a fine line between offering perspectives backed by data and those that are just opinions. Even if we discount this, and assume that everyone contributes with merit, and there are five different perspectives, each backed by its own data, the essential question is, who decides? There can't be five decision makers. We can't vote on every decision. Democracy isn't great for every situation. Sometimes, someone has to swallow the bitter pill, and choose to go in one direction.

I remember being in so many such discussions when running my start-up. It took us days to decide on product names. It took us hours of heated arguments to decide whether to showcase our product value proposition in a three-step or five-step framework. It took us months to decide on hiring one person. Voicing an opinion without context or data started to hurt. Everyone was expected to offer an opinion. Not having one was interpreted as not being interested. So, everyone started to share an opinion for the sake of it, and then we debated every little detail till the cows came home.

In both cases, be it the 'need to know' culture or the 'death by discussions' culture, when there is no incentive for decision making, decision makers will dawdle. Decisions will be delayed not for want of additional information or analysis, but because there is no urgency to move forward, and maintaining the status quo seems a safer option. This, I expect, will be the biggest blocker to adoption when it comes to formulating product strategy.

"With great power comes great responsibility."

— Uncle Ben, Spiderman

A third problem in the culture of organizations is what happens after a decision is taken. How does the follow-through happen? Is there a commitment to see a decision to its end? Is there a blame game? Do we wait for the decision maker to fail to say, "I told you so?" This culture makes decision makers insecure. They lean upon the theory of Agility and make short-sighted decisions to just get over the current problem, assuming that they can change their mind about it. After all, Agility is being able to respond to change. So, teams should be open to decisions being revoked, but Agility is not about constantly changing our mind. Decision making cannot be arbitrary, and without accountability. Remember, we disagree and commit. Teams have to be empowered to access data and information that will help them to make informed choices and have the confidence that stakeholders will commit to decisions that have been taken.

The larger business strategy has to tie directly to product execution. The *Investment Game* is not a fun activity. It is about decision makers exhibiting their intent, and thereby opening themselves up for scrutiny. For this, there needs to be a level of comfort in discussing strategy with the teams that execute the strategy. This brings us to the next aspect of team empowerment.

Collaboration

Strategic planning is not something that all of us do. Reading market trends, visualizing the bigger picture, taking risks, or being willing to let go of a short-term gain to focus on a longer-term impact is not easy. Placing a title on a person does not make them an overnight strategist either!

A great deal of disconnect can happen between teams that execute plans and teams that strategize. This is because the former doesn't get the big picture, and the latter doesn't see the devil in the details. Even when teams have ample freedom to frame and execute their plan of action, they are limited by the brief given to them by someone else who is thinking about strategy. They are essentially working on partial information, and with limited collaboration:

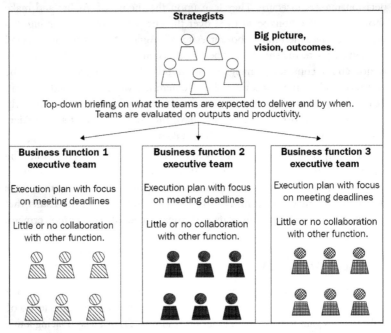

The *Investment Game* and the business value scores establish a forum for the strategic planning teams and the executive teams to align on common outcomes. In an evolving early-stage product, having all hands on board about strategy and execution can be great. Empowered teams can now enjoy complete freedom on *how* to execute their plan to deliver outcomes, while fostering collective ownership of *what* by collaborating with other business functions and understanding the constraints and aspirations of the business, and thereby committing even if they disagree on the *why*.

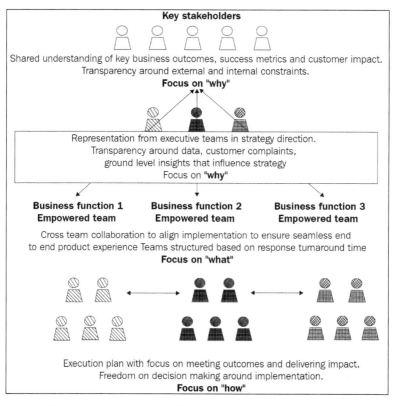

Key stakeholders

Shared understanding of key business outcomes, success metrics and customer impact. Transparency around external and internal constraints.
Focus on "why"

Representation from executive teams in strategy direction.
Transparency around data, customer complaints,
ground level insights that influence strategy
Focus on **"why"**

| Business function 1 | Business function 2 | Business function 3 |
| Empowered team | Empowered team | Empowered team |

Cross team collaboration to align implementation to ensure seamless end to end product experience Teams structured based on response turnaround time
Focus on "what"

Execution plan with focus on meeting outcomes and delivering impact.
Freedom on decision making around implementation.
Focus on "how"

As illustrated in the preceding figure, empowered teams may be teams specializing in one aspect of product building (infrastructure, core engineering, and so on) or a business function (marketing, customer support, and so on). They are empowered to decide on how to execute their plan to meet desired outcomes. There is an organization-wide consensus about Key Business Outcomes, and every team is working collaboratively towards meeting those goals. Each team has representatives who will share the detailed insights from tracking analytics, customer feedback, execution blockers, and other nitty-gritty constraints. Anything that can influence business outcomes will be bubbled up to forums where business outcomes are planned and tracked. This works only if this is a two-way street.

The leadership team must share, with equal rigor, blockers on the larger strategy. They must be able to rationalize a change in vision or business outcomes. At the beginning, teams can be quite uncomfortable when it comes to finding a balance between a five-year vision and a three-month delivery. Relating product strategic goals to day-to-day execution has to become an integral part of how product teams work. Cross-functional collaboration cannot be a luxury. It must remain an essential aspect of how we work. Teams should be enabled to focus on delivering outcomes. They can achieve this by working closely with other business functions. We need to move away from directives to maximize throughput. We need to stop blindly following requirements dictated by strategy teams.

This will require a change in how teams work. Higher collaboration on strategy and execution requires a higher level of Agility in teams. This also means that outcomes, deliverables, and key metrics are shared and easily accessible within the organization. Teams need to be able to adopt and leverage tools that can offer them the flexibility to share information and make goals visible.

Visibility (transparency) and accountability go hand in hand. When everyone is aware of the bigger picture, and the outcomes to pursue, not just success stories but also any failure to meet desired outcomes can be accessible by everyone. Once failures are visible, then fixing accountability ensues. This is another culture smell: when teams think about who to blame instead of what went wrong, and what can we learn from it. The problem is that in such a culture, it is easier to fix accountability on the implementation team rather than on the strategic planning team. It is easier to find fault when you have detailed specs with limited variables. It is hard to define what went wrong when looking at a high-level vision with many variables, many of which seem to not be in our control. This is one of the reasons why teams find it easier to measure output (productivity) instead of outcomes (success metrics). However, the framework of using impact scores enables us to quantify outcomes by comparing actual success metrics with desired outcomes. Unless there is ownership of the why, what, and the how of an Impact Driven Product and high collaboration between stakeholder and business functions, then delivering impact will be at best ad hoc, if not impossible.

Summary

In this book, we learned that lean product management is about empowering teams to collaborate on business outcomes, while consistently tracking progress made toward desired outcomes. It can enable teams to look at an end-to-end product experience by defining the Impact Driven Product. When we lack an understanding about our core company DNA and are unable to visualize what success means for us, we may end up building honeycombs for ants! Empowered teams own execution and strategy. Impact Driven Products are delivered best by teams that understand internal motivations and their core business drivers are aware of internal and external constraints that influence their strategy, and then find the smartest way to deliver an end-to-end satisfying product experience to their customers.

Index

ANOTHER BOOK YOU MAY ENJOY

If you enjoyed this book, you may be interested in another book by Packt:

Understanding Software

Max Kanat-Alexander

ISBN: 978-1-78862-881-5

- ◆ See how to bring simplicity and success to your programming world
- ◆ Clues to complexity - and how to build excellent software
- ◆ Simplicity and software design
- ◆ Principles for programmers
- ◆ The secrets of rockstar programmers
- ◆ Max's views and interpretation of the Software industry
- ◆ Why Programmers suck and how to suck less as a programmer
- ◆ Software design in two sentences
- ◆ What is a bug? Go deep into debugging

Leave a review - let other readers know what you think

Please share your thoughts on this book with others by leaving a review on the site that you bought it from. If you purchased the book from Amazon, please leave us an honest review on this book's Amazon page. This is vital so that other potential readers can see and use your unbiased opinion to make purchasing decisions, we can understand what our customers think about our products, and our authors can see your feedback on the title that they have worked with Packt to create. It will only take a few minutes of your time, but is valuable to other potential customers, our authors, and Packt. Thank you!

www.ingramcontent.com/pod-product-compliance
Lightning Source LLC
Chambersburg PA
CBHW071240050326
40690CB00011B/2203